THE ETHICAL AND EDUCATIONAL COGITATIONS OF BERTRAND RUSSELL AND ALDOUS HUXLEY

Dr. K. Mahendran

Copyright © <2025> <Dr. K. Mahendran>

This book is dedicated to the passionate wings of the thirsty intellects   in search of the pleasurable proximity of the brains of literary sublimity of the past centuries.

Contents

Foreword vii

Preface.. xi

Acknowledgments xiii

Prologue/Introduction...................................... xv

1. Russell's social refirmative concerns ....**Error! Bookmark not defined.**

2. The social refirmative ideas of Huxley 22

3. The ethical views of Bertrand Russell.............. 43

4. The ethical views of Aldous Huxley 54

5. The educational views of Russell ....**Error! Bookmark not defined.**9

6. The educational views of Huxley   92

7. References 102

Foreword

Ethics is the master branch of study from which all other branches of knowledge have branched out. There are two schools of thought on the existence of morality – one school holds that morality is inbuilt and so it is divine, and the other school propagates that it is actually man-made for the disciplined construction of the society so that it will be humane and healthy for the peaceful living of all the people of the society. William Wordsworth says that a mind which is not properly constituted with the branch of philosophy is not a grownup mind at all.

Ethics is the only subject that will stand the test of time and the world will eternally in need of unlike the other subjects and the other subjects are likely to undergo changes and evolutions, but not ethics - the core of ethics shall never loose its sap as to be modified according to the collective strength of the outlaws of anytime. The world needs the raw material called ethics and education in order to create discipline and peace in the society and so it is more important than any brilliant idea towards the sophistication of life in general, since without peace and security in life, any sort of height and supremacy shall consequently meet dilapidation and chaos.

Dr. K. Mahendran's idea to publish the quintessence of the vibrant cogitations of Bertrand Russell and Aldous Huxley on ethics and education for the betterment of the world population is the need of the hour, since the world is already marching towards the scientific advancements, thinking that they are the true identity of lofty living in this world. The more passionate they are towards such materialistic living, the more distanced they are from the core values of life, for which the gift of life has been given to man in general. Ethics is the cardinal Teacher, who speaks with a stern look and voice to make the world fall into the line of discipline as decreed by the Heavens.

Modern man is very proud of his inventions of diabolic and self-destructive scientific inventions, with which human beings make war against one another. It is because the modern man does not know what is power and being powerful. He has replaced the true concept of being powerful with being intimidating to the rest of the world with an inflated pride. Man is the only being that is detrimental to its own species, which he is not ashamed of, because of the incurable frailty and stupidity of being proud about enslaving the rest. Being cruel and dominating, somehow, has creeped into the psychology of the modern man and convinced him that it is the only way to be safe and respectful.

Dr. K. Mahendran has carefully studied the essays of Bertrand Russell and Aldous Huxley and has presented the ethical and educational perspectives with out loosing the original fragrance. It has come out well as a considerable contribution to the already existing books on the ethics and educational ideas of many great thinkers of the past and present. I wish him all the best for the great success of this book and all his future endeavours to contribute to the world of creativity and knowledge.

Dr. G. Sathish,
Assistant Professor of Tamil,
Dr. MGR College of Arts and Science,
Sirkali.

Preface

Ethics and education are the twin pillars upon which any progressive society must stand. As the world confronts increasing moral ambiguity and the erosion of educational values, revisiting the ideas of thinkers who grappled deeply with these themes becomes essential. Among such voices, Bertrand Russell and Aldous Huxley stand out for their enduring insights and critical reflections on humanity's path forward.

Bertrand Russell, a Nobel Prize-winning philosopher, mathematician, and social critic, dedicated much of his life to issues of logic, ethics, education, and peace. Aldous Huxley, best known for his dystopian novel *Brave New World*, was equally a profound essayist and thinker who explored the human condition, the perils of technological advancement, and the role of education in cultivating individual freedom.

This book aims to examine and compare the ethical and educational philosophies of Russell and Huxley. By delving into their writings—both fictional and philosophical—we can better understand their visions of a just society, the nature of human values, and the transformative power of education. Their perspectives, though developed in the 20th century, are strikingly relevant today. From debates on freedom of thought and scientific progress to the moral dilemmas posed by modern education systems, Russell and Huxley offer a rich framework for reflection.

The chapters that follow will first explore the ethical foundations of each thinker, followed by an analysis of their educational theories. The final section offers a comparative study, highlighting where their views align, diverge, and intersect with contemporary issues. In revisiting Russell and Huxley, we not only honor their intellectual legacy but also arm ourselves with critical tools to navigate our own ethical and educational challenges.

Dr. K. Mahendran,
Assistant Professor of English,
SRM IST, Kattankulathur.

Acknowledgments

Acknowledging a few people in my life for whatever productive doings I am into is a part of them, just because they are bound to be the collective force of encouragement for the inception and celebrations when it hits the pinnacle to fly off into the firmament of the completed works of art.

I am very grateful for the departed soul of my mentor **Dr. K. Chellappan,** who propelled my thirst for writing and publishing books by giving foreword to my first book, Swords of Tears.

I express my sincere thanks to my research supervisor **Dr. T. Murugavel,** Professor of English, SVCE, Sriperumpudur.

I am thankful to my friend **Dr. G. Sathish, Professor of Tamil, Dr. MGR College of Arts and Science, Sirkali** for his constant support and encouragement for my intellectual doings in general.

I thank my friend, **Dr. Balamurugan, Professor of English, SRM University,** Kattankulathur for his words of encouragement for all my books and inspiring me with his productive activities.

I thank my friend, **Dr. M. Devendran, Assistant Professor of English, SRM University, Kattankulathur** for his well-wishing and encouragement for my writing books.

I am ever thankful to my **Guru Ragavendirar, Guru Korakkar and the collective Divinity I am associated with** for this spirit of expressions.

Prologue/Introduction

Moral and philosophical reflections on life in general become the rudimentary pavements for the inceptions of the educational journey. Education in general is for the moral preaching so that the people can be properly administered with the well-instilled codes of conducts deep in their psychology. It is only moral preaching through the establishments of education that stands out into spotlight. Morality is the base on which the buildings of the occupationally skilled personality or personal enrichment can be achieved.

Attention itself is the gate of morality with out which nothing can be done satisfactorily. The idea of education is the most productive and all-governing not only in the human world, but also in the animal kingdom, since the skill sets and knowledge of the forefathers are given out the posterity only through the act of demonstration, which is witnessed and imbibed by the young minds of both the human world and the animal kingdom.

The inter-twined state of education and morality is very blatant and so the field of education throughout the world insists on the necessity of being moral and disciplined so that the mind and intellect can be properly built to be highly productive in life. The great thinkers of both the past and present focus more on the moral preachings of the field of education and ethics as a moral sword has been accepted to be the ultimate measure even in scientific inventions. Secured life and peace is the abtract couple, offering the condusive state on this planet to live joyfully and so the idea of education is bound to be dominated by the most intense didactic spirit. This book falls under the category of moral, philosophical and spiritual guidelines much propagated by the humanistic brains across the world. Bertrand Russell and Aldous Huxley have contributed a lot for the idea and refinement of the field of education and this book is the harbinger of them

Russell's social reformative concerns

Russell says that the present condition of the world is pathetic, and it is suffering from two kinds of misfortunes. The first problem is that there are people who genuinely think that the world has to be peaceful and all the people of the world should be comfortable and happy, but cannot contribute anything to those who suffer and the second misfortune is that there are people, who have what those who suffer terribly are in need of, but do not offer. Russell says that the second type of people want to make a huge profit out of their surplus goods.

Russell says that the surplus of coffee in Brazil is used as a fuel on the railways, and it is burnt in large funeral pyres in the lonely valleys of the county. There is a gut of rubber because the workers of the country cannot help taking rubber from the trees and that it was stopped by the pest attacked the rubber trees. He says that in the past the weevil that affected the cotton production is now regarded a heaven-sent gift or cure for the human carelessness in producing the surplus amount of something, which is not properly planned for the usage, but wasted by using for unproductive purposes out of a touch of indifference. He says:

> The world at the present day is suffering from two misfortunes: there are people who desire good which they cannot purchase, and there are people who have goods

which they cannot sell. Those who
have goods which they cannot sell
are adopting various ingenious
means of disposing of their surplus.
IT would be demoralizing to wage
earners to pay wages for work not
done; therefore, they continue to
produce the good that they cannot
sell but adopt various means of
destroying them after they have been
produced. Brazil, which suffers from
a surplus of coffee, has taken to
using it as fuel on the railways and to
burning it on large funeral pyres in
lonely valleys. There is a glut of
rubber, which is unfortunately made
worse by the fact that the natives
cannot be restrained from tapping the
rubber trees. (MO: 54)

Russell says that anything very significantly
useful, which is produced out of the sheer toiling
and human squandering of energy, must not be
either wasted or misused to get a false gratification
that it is, after all, used for some purpose. He says
that the habit of doing some productive tasks is
deeply instilled in the human psychology that man
cannot not but find pleasure in involving himself in
some productive activities, which he associates with
a sense of pride and usefulness. He not only has this
inclination towards doing some work, but also the
most efficient ways of doing it, since the clear
display of efficiency in doing something sets forth
the doer at a supreme level and his endeavour to do

something in a special way is greatly wondered and appreciated. Others are also deeply inspired by the height of capacity at which some productive assignment is dealt with.

Russell says that every producer of some products must think of the truth that it going to be both fruitful and bring joy for the user or consumer. Russell says that the morality of work, throughout the world, is very intense and the world follows it strictly, since it considers work as something divine, which actually has established a world system that has witnessed half of the world being poor because of its overproduction and the other half is also poor, since it consumes little. He says:

> The habit of work has become ingrained in the greater part of the human species and not only the habit of work but, what is worse, the habit of looking for ways by which work can be made more productive. Nobody has thought for a moment that it might be a good thing if somebody could enjoy the produce of human labour. Our morality is ascetic, which makes us regard work as a virtue; it follows that production is good and consumption is bad. This ascetic twist has produced a world system in which half the world is poor because it produces too much and the other half because it consumes too little. (MO: 54)

Russell says that this attitude of being not careful about the limit of the production of something, which is the intelligent way of avoiding regrettable wastage and improper usages, is insane and therefore it must be seriously strategized to preserve what has been produced by hard labour and to prevent destroying life-giving resources of Nature. Russell in a very funny way says that the boll weevil that eats at cotton would say, if asked, that the purpose of cotton production is misunderstood and that it is not for the production of dress material for human beings, but for giving nourishment for their species and that it would even go to the extent of complaining that cotton is a very velvety and delicious substance and it is unfortunately spoiled by the nasty perspiration of human beings.

Thank you so much this weekthe weevil, are to get enough nourishment, happiness and freedom, which are severely hampered by the nasty human cruelty. He says:

> What is the cure for this queer insanity? If we could ask the advice of the boll weevil and the rubber pest, they would have a ready answer. The boll weevil would say: 'you have radically misconceived the purpose of cotton; it does not exist to clothe human beings but to supply nourishment to the boll weevil. Human beings', so I am afraid it might continue, 'have in any case not much to be said for them, and it is

unworthy of a pleasant substance such as cotton to be condemned to absorb their perspiration. The boll weevil, on the contrary, fights no wars, has no police force, and does not teach the multiplication table to its young. Clearly, therefore, the sum of sentient happiness in the terraqueous globe will be increased if the boll weevil replaces man. (MO: 55)

Russell says that there is enough logic and intelligence in the argument of the weevil and man may reject the argument out of his partiality, pride and selfishness. Russell says that if man is to refute the logic of the insect, he has to behave sensibly like the insect at least. The insect consumes the cotton, whenever it wants and does not think of hiding it for other benefits and profits like human beings. Human beings keep the goods in one place and the future customers in another place, calling it a bad trade to overcome this huddle and to improve trade, the gap between the goods and the want of the customers must be beneficially bridged, with the understanding and acceptance that each operation at each moment may not be profitable. Russell says:

Perhaps we, as human beings, may be allowed enough partiality for our species to reject this argument. But it is not enough merely to reject it, we ought not to be outdistanced in logic by this humble insect. If we are to refute him, we must behave at least

as sensibly as he does. He consumes
the cotton when he wants it whereas
we keep the cotton in one place and
the would-be customers in another;
we then complain of bad trade. It
seems clear that to improve trade, we
must find some way of bringing
goods to those who want them. So
far, however, the collective wisdom
of mankind has not been equal to this
effort. (MO: 55)

Bertrand Russell comes out with his profusion of humanism through the exhibition of his worry that many downtrodden, unemployed and forsaken population of this world are into starvation and the concern that they must be given enough food to the languishing population to make them feel that they are also living in this world at least with the basic requirements to be joyfully alive. He says that the rotting food in the West America and Canada could be given to those people of starvation around the industrial regions so that the world would be really richer, and this can be achieved at the cost of the inhuman profits of the individual capitalist. This is possible only by an organized public endeavour and the humanistic motive of which will be unstoppably undeniable. Russell recommends:

There is food rotting in the West of
the United States and Canada; there
are unemployed populations starving
in   all   he   industrial   regions

6

throughout the world. If the food were brought to the starving populations, and they were set to wok such as would satisfy the wants of Western farmers, the world would be the richer even I no individual capitalist made a profit. The motive of individual profit has apparently broken down, and only organized public effort will restore the economic life of the world. (MO: 55)

Bertrand Russell talks about the pathetic condition of the world due to the mental, emotional and intellectual decay, which the majority of the modern population is least bothered about. Russell says that a hundred and fifty years ago, the rich people were truly civilized. A rich man of those days, he says, was expected to quote Latin poets, to judge Italian Renaissance pictures and appreciate classical music and so a man of the period had a considerable knowledge about the literature of his country and France. In the modern times, such expectations are only with professors, and it is so awful that it is restricted to academic departments.

Russell says that such activities are not very serious nowadays because he does not find any necessity to know the names of muses or the signs of the zodiac, but they were taught to his grandparents, which they remembered even at their eighties. He says that the modern world does not find any leisure because their sense of pleasure has become very tiresome as their work, resulting in the increase of cleverness and decrease of wisdom, because modern man does not find time to meditate on a thought so intensely as to have distilled wisdom out of it. He says:

> The result is that while cleverness has increased, wisdom has decreased because no one has the time for the slow thoughts out of which wisdom, drop by drop, is distilled. A problem such as the prevention of war, the urgency of which is obvious to everyone, is dismissed with a shrug of the shoulders in the hope that circumstances will solve it without the aid of human thought. But circumstance, unaided, are not likely to be so kind. (MO:35)

Russell says that it is the reason why the majority of the people of the world is indifferent to the greatest thought like the prevention of war, the most urgent idea to be executed. Mere circumstances will not solve it without the serious and careful human efforts. Russell mocks at the quakers stating that they instilled in the minds of the people that the practice of half an hour of silent meditation will give people enough physical and mental strength to do their personal, national and international works efficiently. He says, "Two minutes a year, on Armistice Day, are given to silence, and all the other minutes of the year to largely futile bustle. The proportion is wrong; if the silence were longer, the bustle would be less futile."

(MO: 35) Russell aims at bringing in a sea-change in the minds of the people of the world to be sensible and clear about their personal, social and political responsibilities, through pointing out both their petty and inexcusable mistakes.

Russell has chosen the frailty of the modern people to seek admiration in other people in the society to shed some intellectual light on. He wants the people of the world not to seek their comfort and peace of mind outside of themselves, since the secret of joy and peace lies with their state of mind. He says that though many people are under the impression that they are living only to the contentment of their conscience and do not pay attention to the opinion of others, the majority of the people of the world seeks to impress others and tries hard to get their admiration. Russell says that only a few do not care for the opinion of others, and they are the real heroes.

Russell says that it is important to observe whose admiration people desire to attain. An average man has the aspiration to get the respect from his colleagues, wife, children and subordinates. He is so strong that his business associates must think that he is very special and capable that they must have an eternal respect and admiration for him, but he never minds knowing how well his wife and children love him and tries to persuade himself that during a crisis his children would come to him to seek his advice. He says:

> The average man desires the respect
> of his colleagues, of his wife and

children (if possible), and of his underlings. He hopes that his business associates do not consider him a simple fellow whom anybody could take in. He takes pains not to realize how well his wife knows him. He tries to persuade himself that in a crisis his children would turn to him for advice. The average married woman tries to impress other married women. She tries to persuade them that her husband is richer than theirs and her children more successful. If she is well-to-to, she tries to display better taste than her neighbours in the management and decoration of her house. As they are playing the same game, this requires great skills and much thought. (MO: 50)

The spirit to impress these people does not yield even if it encounters difficulties in impressing many or some. He comes out with the example of the writers, Bronte sisters and says that even though their books have attained acclaim and love, their personalities are such that they never try to impress their neighbours. Russell comes out with some examples of great men who were driven by the spirit of impressing others.

Anatole France's Pontius Pilate convinced himself that the posterity will understand him and get him justice after his death, when he incurred the ranker of the emperor. Julius Caesar had Alexander the Great as his rival in his mind, in spite of the glorious victories he had. The eminent men of the past lived with the intention of living forever in the minds of the people of the world even after their death.

Russell remembers an Italian business magnate, who was on his death bed under the impression that he had not enough fame or place in the pages of history said that he missed the chance of murdering the Pope and the Emperor at once that would get him a place in history. He says that such a desire to be immortalized in the pages of history of the world has been decreased thanks to the newspapers of the present days. The contemporary fame and the possibility of being famous through newspapers is more intense and greater than the expected fame of a person in the pages of the history and so today's world knows that the possible admiration from the readers of history is less than the contemporary fame that one could possibly get now. Russell indirectly expresses his discontentment and amazement when he says that the fame of a film star, at the height of his career, in the present day exceeds even Alexander the Great and Julius Caesar's. He says:

> The fame of a film star at the present ay far exceeds that of Alexander or Caesar at the height of his career. Probably more people know the name of Einstein now than have known the name of Archimedes in all the centuries from his day to our

own. The effect of all this is that admiration is sought in more ephemeral forms than those formerly desired. Men's work becomes less statuesque and there is more effort to make it appeal to all and sundry. (MO: 51)

He says that the possibility of getting instant fame throughout the world is very much and that is the reason why the number of people who know Einstein is more when compared with how many know of Archimedes in all the centuries from his days and says that the admiration of the modern world is ephemeral than how was it in the past. The desire for posthumous fame lingers in almost all very prominent men along with the fear of having something bad in their biography and so they are afraid of their biographers and as a result, in the life of eminent people hypocrisy has replaced spontaneity. Bertrand Russell says that admiration is not offered to what is truly admirable and those who are admired do not deserve it.

Marriage is an interesting subject to all throughout the world and Bertrand Russell recollects the driver of the car he was travelling by turning back and asking whether he was Bertrand Russell and said that he used to listen to his lectures and has stopped such intellectual activities since his marriage. Russell says that marriage, which is expected to make anyone become complete and fulfilled, unfortunately attributed to unhappiness. He says that the actual reason lies partly both with economics and social custom. He says that the conventional idea that husband and wife should spend their leisure time together is not an intelligent idea.

Russell continues to say that his taxi driver's wife does not have any taste for intellectual lectures and does not like him also to enjoy the lecture without her company. Russell says that many husbands and wives are ready to sacrifice their pleasures on the jealousy of the pleasures of their partners and calls it dangerous to object and prevent other people's pleasure out of jealousy than to be selfish about pursuing one's own. He says that if a husband and wife are to be compatible and happy, there must be some sort of social separateness. Russell says:

> The convention that husbands and wives should spend their leisure hours together is a bad one. No doubt my taxi driver's wife does not care for lectures and does not like him to go to them without her. Many husbands and many wives will forgo their own pleasures out of jealousy of their pleasures that they imagine that their partners as desiring. It is much more harmful to object to other people's pleasures than it is to be a trifle selfish in pursuing one's own, and a certain amount of social separateness of husband and wife is necessary if they are not to become

dull and incapable of finding anything to say to each other. (MO: 36)

The second reason, economic difficulty, is more serious, he says and that an unmarried man, unlike a married man, is free to be lavish about his money for his leisure time and amusement, including searching for a wife. He says that well-educated and intellectual married men will find that their freedom and leisure time for intellectual pursuits have vanished and educated, and intellectual women are bound to feel the loss of freedom and time to explore the world of intellect more intensely than men do, if they remain childless and as a result both have some feeling against the institution of marriage. Russell says that this problem cannot be cured unless the state undertakes the entire expense of children.

Russell says that this condition can be effectively changed with the adoption of an intelligent attitude towards childrearing. Bertrand Russell says that child-rearing is a very responsible act, since it is a calling for cultivating a great set of skills, giving chance to interesting observation and taking them to the world of science. He says that when compared with affection, science and other skills and intelligence are of no use and nothing can replace affection and that science, and the acquired skills should supplement affection. If not, it will produce unexpected dangerous results. He says that he is sure that intellectuals will never see marriage in an admirable light, if they come to realize the scientific interest of infancy.

Russell declares to the world that an ignorant person blessed with a rich affection is better than a very intelligent and knowledgeable person with no heart, but a well-informed person being fond of children, is the better state to have children. Russell impliedly says that a man with an enriched heart is more desirable than a man with an enriched brain. He says, "The ignorant person with affection is perhaps better for an infant than a well-informed person who has no heart; but a well-informed person who is fond of children is much better than either." (MO: 37) He embraces and reflects the ideas of the Greek philosopher, Aristotle, who says that educating the mind without educating the heart is no education at all. The societal well-being depends on the human qualities of the people ultimately, though a society becomes advanced with the help of human brains.

Russell talks about the modern parenting and the incompatible method of teaching children at schools and colleges. Russell says that he is against the popular belief that all parents love their children, because they show their love through being very strict about their activities and expressions. In the name of teaching discipline, they are told that whatever they do are wrong. Children are not allowed to be children, and they are given the feeling that whatever is taught does not permit them to be free and happy. Russell says that majority of the parents are very strict with their children because they know not of the modern child psychology. He says:

> Now character is mainly determined before the age of six, when schooling begins. If the state understood modern child psychology, it would make all children go to nursery school from the age of two onward. There the child would find an environment composed of other children, with a grown-up in the background who would unobtrusively give a sense of safety. There would be no prohibition of noise and movement; there would be a minimum of dangers to be guarded against; and there would be as few things forbidden as a carefully arranged environment would make possible. (MO: 43)

Bertrand Russell talks of the deceptive appearance of the American Society that it gives importance to women's emancipation and that women have achieved equality. He says that the ideal of America is equality from the beginning of the history of the declaration of American Independence. He says that manufacturers, landowners, railway mines and oil trade have made some people so rich that they have become very important persons to influence the important affairs of their countries. They are blessed with technology and immense knowledge and technique about the economy in general that no force against inequality can possibly defeat them.

Even though America brags about its ideal of equality, it has used its ideal only in some compatible political directions and not in the society. Social equality is the basic necessity that every citizen of a country needs in order to experience the fundamental freedom and joy of life. This American ideal has not been experienced by the people, especially Negro men and women. Still, they are considered inferior to the white race and the black Americans undergo insults and oppressions in the society, even though, the political ideology of the country strongly condemns such oppressions.

Russell says that women have political equality with men, but not economic equality, which is very important for women in the modern world to be independent and feel confident about their constructive sides. The wife of a rich man will have enough money to spend, but the women of other classes depend on their earning husbands for money. The women, according to the law, have their rights to share the income of their husbands, but still it is unfortunate that the true emancipation, economic independency, of women has not been attained. Russell says:

> Although equality was, from the moment of the Declaration of Independence, proclaimed as a principle, it was only applied in such directions as were politically

convenient. For a long time, nobody thought of it as including Negroes or women. Even now, although women have political equality with men, they do not, as a rule, have, economic equality, which is in many ways more important. Among the rich, a wife normally has money of her own, but in other classes she depends upon her husband's earnings. The law gives her a right to a share of his income, and to alimony when she gets tired of him or he of her; but it does not give her the economic power that belongs to the person who earns money. (MO: 269)

Russell says that the American women seem to be more powerful than men to the foreign onlookers, when they look at the rich people of the country, but it is deceptive because women are more powerful than men only in the fields in which men are not given the first preference. He says that the power of love of a business man finds its outlet in his office itself and so, he can be free of his business plans and strategies, when he is at home, reserving them all to himself and enjoy the home atmosphere, which is more important to the country than his dependency of his wife, when it comes to the household activities.

Women do not like this attitude and so they are of the opinion that business is for those who are not so refined and for very sensitive men. Women, as they think of business in this way, tend to underestimate the significance of earning money, without understanding that the economic reality is at war with the pretention that women enjoy economic equality, and they are superior to men. This attitude leads to the psychological satisfaction about their superiority complex and imaginary status. This pretention leads to giving superficial importance to feminine culture, in the name of respecting or even regarding them as superior parts of the society. Russell says:

> With this goes, quite naturally, a tendency to underestimate the importance of the economic side of life, since the economic reality is at war with the social presence of women's equality or even superiority. Acceptance of this pretence gives, as acceptance of pretence always does, a certain superficiality and unimportance to much feminine culture, besides having a regrettable effect upon the psychology of women." (MO: 270)

Russell says that the concept of democracy is not very clear, when there is a confusion between quality among classes and equality between men and women. This inequality will continue to exist as long as it is political and not economic. The right to vote against someone politically is just a consolation given to women. Russell says that political democracy must exercise its power to suppress any evil force in the society, causing imbalance and must execute the distribution of economic power. He says that political justice cannot be achieved, without achieving economic justice and neither of them is complete without the other, which was recognized by the founders of the country, but their plan of creating several independent economic units is not available in the industrial age. He says:

> Democracy, whether taken as equality between classes or as equality between men and women, has not much reality so long as it is merely political and not also economic. It is small consolation to be able to vote against a political programme, if its advocates have the power to make you starve. Political democracy has its importance, since it prevents certain extremes of oppression, and is a necessary step towards the more equitable distribution of economic power. But without economic justice, political justice is incomplete. This was more or less recognized by the founders of American Democracy, but their method, which was the creation of vast numbers of independent economic units is no longer available in our industrial age. (MO: 270)

Russell, in the pretext of talking for the economic equality of women in the western world, talks for it for the women of the entire world. He makes a very strong statement, "The battle for economic democracy will be the next great struggle for justice in human affairs." (MO: 270) The society that Russell aspires to establish has the characteristic qualities of an ideal society. He wants the people to be free from any sort of fear and grow confident and brave. People should be well-educated, rational and humanistic with free operations of intellect so that they will be courageous enough to be revolutionary, whenever they find any obstacle for the healthy function of the society. Peter Stone in his book, *So You Want to Read Bertrand Russell*, says, "A society dedicated to Russell's radical liberal principles required citizens who were fearless, thoughtful, ready and willing to challenge authority, sceptical of dogma, respectful of other human beings regardless of nationality or creed." (22) Peter stone has encapsulated the major socio-political ideas of Bertrand Russell in all these words.

The social reformative concerns of Aldous Huxley

The Huxleyan social reformative ideas are for the individual refinements of the people of the world to be strong and responsible about their socio-political contributions for their countries. Huxley says that there are many definitions of an ideal society, and he wants to give a humanistic definition of an ideal society, which all men and women would find acceptable. He says that a humanist is the one who believes that human nature should be harmoniously developed and that the sacrifices man makes should be done out of his highest interest for the well-being of the entire humanity and not due to anything supernatural or out of anything humane. He says:

The humanist is one who believes that our human nature can, and should be, developed harmoniously as a whole – that the sacrifices which man must always make should be made in his own highest interest, and not in the interest of something external to himself – not in the name of any less or any more than human cause. (BW: 107)

According to a humanist, Huxley says, the members of an ideal society are superior in quality physically, intellectually and morally. The society is impeccable in establishing morality in all possible realms that no one will be treated unjustly, and no talent goes unrecognised. It becomes the embodiment of personal liberty and at the same time garlands and eulogises any altruistic efforts, it is not stagnant, but purposefully dynamic, drifting towards the realization of lofty human aspirations.

He says that science should be used to build such a society and the powers of science should be used by humanistic rulers. He says:

> For the humanist, then, the ideal society is one whose constituent members are all physically, intellectually and morally of the best quality; a society so organised that no individual shall be unjustly treated or compelled to waste or bury his talents; a society which gives its members the greatest possible amount of individual liberty, but at the same time provides them with the most satisfying incentives to altruistic effort; a society not static but deliberately progressive, consciously tending towards the realization of the highest human aspirations. Science must be made a means for the creation of such a society, but only on certain conditions: that the powers which science offers must be used by rulers who are fundamentally humanist. (BW: 107)

Aldous Huxley says that the present crisis is due to instability in economy, which is because of the commercial attitudinal rule that eventually wants to turn the world into a big supermarket there by devastating the just tastes and wants of the people around the world. He says that mechanisation stands for mass production and mass production leas to preparation of a very wide market with a great number of people with flexible needs and tastes. He says that stability and uniformity are the pre-requisites for any rational plan for improving the quality of civilization. The aim of such destructive economists would be for mass-producers and mass-consumers. Huxley says that this is dangerous and so once stability is achieved in economy, scientific research should not be encouraged because nothing is more dangerous than too much of knowledge. He says,

> "So long as scientific research goes on, society stands poised above a potential succession of earthquakes. Any day some new discovery may make all existing equipment obsolete, may revolutionize all existing technique, or else, by changing man's physiological habits, radically alter his whole way of thinking and feeling." (BW: 108)

He says that humanist rulers should not allow the application of some discovery, even though they are for some good purpose, for example the production of synthetic food. He says that one of the branches of science is the field of psychology which is going to be used to distract the attention of people around the world and to persuade the collective attitude of people towards something destructive. He says that such knowledge has already been applied very intelligently on the connection between the people's attitude and the problems of governments. Huxley talks of the possibilities of certain things which sound both remote and as predictions. When he talks of how science is going to influence and the condition of human beings in general, he says that the field of psychology is going to be misused on man as to condition him according to governments in future. He remembers Sigmund Fraud's discovery that the events in the first three months of a new born child decide how the child's personality is going to be as an adult and that the governments in future will invent an idea to implement this sort of mutations in the collective attitude and personality of the population on this earth and decide how should they react to whatever the governments decide and take actions against anything. Aldous says:

> They may succeed in creating a great world-wide community united by common beliefs and aspirations, common wants, tastes and thoughts. It will be a Holy Roman Empire minus the holiness, a Christendom, but without the Christianity – or if nominally Christian, Christian in a way that neither the primitive convert, nor the mediaeval Catholic, nor the later Protestant would recognise as Christian. It will be the kingdom of industry and the machine. (BW: 111)

This is the reason why Huxley is against scientific propaganda, and he says that the idea of a humanist will just be incompatible with a small or large group of people who have the tendency to thraldom, war and bloodshed. He says, "Now personal liberty is, for the humanist, something of the highest value. He believes that, on the whole, it is better to 'go wrong in freedom than to go right in chains' – even if the chains are imponderable, even

if they are not felt by the prisoner to be chains."
(BW: 111) He says that the field of applied bio-
chemistry, pharmacology and drugs can be used in
order to change man's character, temperament and
intelligence as to be suitable to the governments. He
says:

> I will add a few more words by way of
> summary and epilogue. Science in itself is
> morally neutral; it becomes good or evil
> according as it is applied. Ideally, science
> should be applied by humanists. In this case
> it would be good. In actual fact, it is more
> likely to be applied by economists, and so to
> turn out, if not wholly bad, at any rate a very
> mixed blessing. It rests with us and our
> descendants to decide whether we shall use
> the unprecedented power which science
> gives us for good or for bad purposes. It is in
> our hands to choose wisely or unwisely.
> Alas, that wisdom should be so much harder
> to come by than knowledge! (BW: 114)

Huxley talks about the evil nature of
swindling and corruption in a country. He says that
when crime is lucrative, there is an inadequate
punishment and the increase in the number of the
criminals is rambunctious. When there is a
combination of swindling and corruption in a
country, it leads to the undue domination of those
who are economically rich. Economic progress and
democratic government on liberal principles lead to
large-scale swindling and criminal corruption of
politicians. Huxley says that economic progress,

liberal government and corruption practices are unavoidably interconnected.

Huxley says that economic progress is possible only by those who are resourceful and inventive. Such people are interested in creating something that could bring in a change to the society and they are flexible to embrace any change, and this group comprises of only a minority in the world. Most of the people of the world does not welcome change. Change in any form is herculean and excruciating to them and they worship sentiments, but not logic, being fanatical about believing in metaphysical absolutes. The first group of people are driven by the spirit of leading, while the second group is dominated by mere sentiments. Huxley says that the second category of people stand for stability, aggressiveness and the timeliness of an action directed by rash faith in an absolute.

The frailty of this group of people is its inability to adopt to any new change or condition and its attitude towards economic and mental stagnation, unlike the first group of people. Huxley says, "Thus, the strength of a society dominated by men with a pronounced 'persistence of aggregates' likes in its stability and in the violence and the promptitude of the actions dictated by unquestioning faith in an absolute. Its weaknesses are its inability to adapt itself to new conditions and its tendency to economic and mental stagnation." (BW: 143) Huxley glorifies this group of people stating that these men were responsible for the economic growth of the last two centuries, which has necessitated their becoming of the parts of the ruling class. He says that the strength of faith is so intense in the people, who belong to the group of 'persistence of aggregates' and the danger is that men will be rash about enforcing conformity through violence, where there is a strong faith. Huxley says that the noble blood of a martyr is the fertile seed of the Church, and the blood of a nonconformist is unavoidable. Huxley says:

> Now, where the 'persistence of aggregates' is strong, faith is strong; and where faith is strong, men have no hesitation in using violence to enforce conformity to their will. The blood of the martyrs is the seed of the Church; the blood of the heretics is its inevitable fruit. Absolutism in government is correlated with absolutism in philosophy and religion; both are the products of faith, of the persistence of aggregates of sentiments. (BW: 144)

Huxley says that there are strength and weakness in both the group, but the undesirable weakness about being manipulated, using the spirit for loyalty and emotional nature is very much with the second group. Huxley says that fascists and communists encourage 'persistence of aggregates' against the mental freedom of the people of this category. Huxley's humane concern is revealed here, when he talks of the two groups of people in the society. He glorifies, but does not condemn the other, because he is sympathetic towards their weakness to be misused for by the selfishness and pride of the powerful people in the world and so he alerts the group.

Huxley points out the fact that man has a well-cherished pride that he is civilized and has developed his intellectual faculties to that extent that there is nothing to be included or developed hereafter, but unfortunately, the modern man is out of the healthy order and discipline. He does not know what is right and wrong and indulges in the capricious process of pleasure-seeking, which ultimately has made him blind on quality, virtues and true strengths in life. Huxley makes a clear-cut distinction between the barbarians and the modern people, quoting the philosopher, Thomas Hobbes, stating that the life of a savages is very untidy and deplorably nasty. Their life involves brutal activities like hunting, and they don't have longevity. The civilized people are clean, speak very well and they are blessed with a good and satisfactory life span. Huxley says that the price which the civilized people have given for being not savages is heavy. It is only civilization which has produced powerful and deadly weapons of mass destruction, the deadly cancer, the pitiable slums and newspapers. Huxley writes:

> The English philosopher, Thomas Hobbes, was doubtless right; the life of savages is "nasty, solitary, brutish, and short." But the life of civilized men --- however hygienic, relatively speaking, and long --- is not all beer and skittles. Fate makes no free gifts; it sells, for a price. The price is heavy.

Machine guns, cancer, sums, the penny
newspaper --- these are a few items of the
tribute we pay to fate for the privilege of not
being savages. It would be easy to lengthen
the list. In this place, however, I shall
confine myself to a description of one of the
minor horrors of civilisation --- but a minor
horror which, if it were not, providentially,
escapable, would certainly deserve to be
styled a major drawback to civilised life. I
refer to what is called politesociety. (AHCE:
388)

Huxley says that the leisured society must
be avoided, since it has nothing to do with anything
really constructive. This society is of two parts and
the essence or the by-products of the activities of
both the parts are just the same. Huxley says that
both the divisions of this society cannot tolerate the
easy and simple existence, which is a vacuum for
them that they try to fill with useless activities. The
means by which these two groups attain this futility
is different. The first group of people are simple,
children-like, very happy and unspoilt barbarians.
They involve in courting, paring, separating,
repairing, nest-making, birdwatching and games.
The second group of people are into many activities
in the name of being readers, intellectuals, and
aesthetic people. Huxley says:

So much for good society of the lower
browed variety. What now of the highbrow
rich, the aristocratic intellectuals, the
leisured patrons of the arts? What of these?

They ought, of course, by definition to be superior to the lowbrows. Experience, alas, gives the lie to a priori definitions. I am inclined to think that, on the whole, the highbrows are almost worse than the lows. Those who sin after having seen the light and eaten of the tree of knowledge are more blameworthy than those who sin in pre-Adamite innocence and darkness. (AHCE: 389)

Huxley justifies why the second group has to be punished. He says that the Adam, who has committed a sin after eating the fruit of knowledge is more punishable than the Adam, who committed a sin in all his divine innocence. Being intellectuals is severely misunderstood by the second group, Huxley says that and all that they do, in the name of intellectual activities, is only displaying how much they know about how many things. Huxley talks of the salon spectacles of the respective groups. The first group comes to their salon for public house party and drawing room visits and the second group comes to their salon to meet interesting people and talk. Huxley says that they talk of the latest pictures, scandals, pornographies, eccentricities, the latest books, modes, music, religions, psychologies of love, theories of science and philosophy. Huxley severely attacks these activities and calls them futile. He says that these activities are very agreeable and diverting, but it is a very deeply shocking and unthinkably horrible, if it is taken really seriously.

Huxley is angry on this particular group because he says that art is only another killer of time like playing any game or any romantic flirtation to the people of this group. Religion, for them, is something to be talked about over tea or coffee. They consider religion to be an entertaining subject and not so amusing like scandals. Huxley says that they degrade all important and significant ideas and they have turned all values upside down. They value intellectually talking men and ideas very high, nor for their inbuilt merits, but because of their projected merits which are highly fashionable for them. Huxley is very sorry that literature is just a game of elegance for them and have distanced the true merits of getting associated with the soul of literature. He says:

> In highbrow salons, on the other hand, you must talk --- of the latest pictures, the latest scandals, pornographies, and eccentricities, the latest books, the latest modes; the latest music, the latest religions, the latest psychologies of love, the latest theories of science and philosophy. And it is all, no doubt, very agreeable and diverting; but oh, if you happen to take anything at all seriously, how profoundly shocking and horrible! For to these polished beings, art is only another time killer, like bridge and flirtation; religion is something to be lightly chatted about over the tea and muffins --- an amusing subject, but not, of course, so entertaining as a juicy piece of scandal. All fine and important things are degraded; all

values are overturned. Men and ideas are prized in this polite society, not for their intrinsic merit, but because they happen, for one reason or another, to be fashionable. Literature is turned into a sort of elegant game, in which it is the object of the players to score points of 'style' and 'form' --- as though form and style possessed and real existence apart from substance. (AHCE: 389-390)

Huxley talks of the methods by which the world can be improved and comes out with interesting suggestions to ameliorate the life on this planet. He says that the world that the people are living in is man-made and there are only a few in the world, which cannot be created by man. He begins with nurturing the body and talks of the importance of nutritious food for all and says that man is doing so many things, which are highly destructive to his body and does not take care of it, due to his following of stupid customs and other social impositions. Huxley says, "Take, for example, the all-important matter of diet. A science of nutrition exists, but are its precepts followed? They are not. Half the population is too poor to be able to feed itself properly. (The remedy for this is in the hands of the economic planners.) The other half possesses the means but neglects the available knowledge and eats either excessively or mistakenly." (BW: 221) It reflects that modern man is either excessive or improper in almost everything that he deals with, and the implied meaning is that he is away from even the basic discipline and responsibilities.

Huxley says that the newspaper has a considerable space for the advertisement for laxatives, cold-cures, pain killers and ick-me-ups. It is because of not being careful about taking nutritious food and paying enough attention and care to one's body in general. All these are very harmful drugs and the need for the usages of these drugs originates from the modern man's ignorance about the importance about his body, as a result, the body invites many ailments. Man poisons his body with wrong foods and then needs painkillers to reduce the pain he cannot tolerate. Huxley says that man poisons his body and then in the name of mitigating the pains the poison causes, he further pollutes his body with those painkillers.

Then he complains that life is not worth living and consequently starts blaming the government of his country. He says, "We poison ourselves with the wrong food, then try to mitigate the painful consequences of our folly by poisoning ourselves still further with drugs. After which we wonder why it is that life should seem so little worth living and proceed to blame the Government." (BW: 221) Huxley says that there are factories manufacturing these drugs with efficient machines and with the help of intelligent scientists, but the purpose of these drugs is to temporarily fight the pain and reduce the effect of the other poisons with a less poisonous substance at a cheap rate. Huxley is against pains and inflicting pains on anyone and so he talks about preventing this painful state before they occur so that there would be no necessity for such factories to produce harmful drugs, which depends on man's carefulness towards his body and physical well-bring.

The next idea that Huxley suggests improving the world is to eradicate the deadly habit of taking intoxicants, stimulants and sedatives. He says that the actual reason behind this particular problem is psychological. Man needs occasional holiday or break to escape the hard realities of life. It is a tragedy that the people of the world spends the ten percent of their total income on intoxicating, stimulating and sedative materials. Huxley says that the habit of taking tea and tobacco also is out of the need to escape the reality or boredom. He says:

> A problem closely allied to that of analgesics, and no less important to us as suffering and enjoying beings, is the problem of intoxicants, stimulants and sedatives. Everywhere and always men have felt the need of taking an occasional holiday from the common round of every-day affairs – a holiday from the world and should guess that, at the present time, the inhabitants of our planet spend nearly ten percent of their total income on intoxicants, stimulants and sedatives. Some of these – tea, for example, and are exceedingly powerful drugs. But the purpose served by all of them is the same; people take them in order to escape from the boring or unpleasant reality of their own

characters and the surrounding world. (BW: 225)

Huxley says that man has to adapt to the surroundings and must lead a happy life so that the need for escaping realities and boredom will start diminishing. Life has to be improved in such a way that it becomes very interesting and truly valuable, which will be a real cure for the weakness to think of slipping into an unreal world of dirty and harmful pleasures. Huxley says, "If we can arrange our world in such a way that people's lives will seem to them worth living, there will be a smaller demand for pick-me-up and stupefacients, for booze and dope." (BW: 225) Huxley says that the children must be taught the skills or art of concentrating on something so as to delve deep into anything to explore many things and such intensity of concentration itself is a powerful tool that can be used both for doing a work efficiently and for the personal benefit of constructively diverting one's attention from something boring or disturbing, the practice of which will present the children from following the psychological means to escape anything painful, which is not an art, but a mere distractions that does not enable the children to cure their shortcomings. Huxley says that the advanced areas of science must not be used to nourish the irresponsibility. He says:

> We teach our children none of the techniques of mental concentration and meditation, by means of which it is possible for the individual to escape, by purely

psychological means, from the distractions of ordinary life, to forget for a moment an even permanently to transcend the shortcomings of his character. And at the same time we permit irresponsible individuals to use all the resources of applied science in order to tell us lies and to fill our minds with ideas which are either ignoble or idiotic. (BW: 226)

Huxley points out the dreadful effects of watching movies and popular press to escape boredom. He says that seeking these means takes the watchers to a world of fantasy distanced from reality, truth, good sense and human values. Huxley says that these means that take people far away from truth is like the political propaganda used by rich men in a democratic country for their financial benefits and the dictators doing the same with people's mind, creating anarchy. Huxley says that the media of a country has to be honest to publish only what is true about anything, which is the basic need for the true improvement of the world. He strictly says that the popular literature of the world has to be useful to the people like the electric power and transport.

There should be a corporation to monitor the desirability of the content to be given to the people, which includes the comments of the writers on political parties also. News must be bought by the corporation for the monitory benefit of the fetchers so that their dependence on advertisement for their money can be eliminated. The officially appointed editors will be meticulous and careful about ignoring anything worthless and harmful for the public and improper material from getting published. With all these precautious purification of news in general is very much possible with which false propaganda can be curbed. Huxley says that this is the only effective measure to protect the common people from the purposefully enforced vulgarity, which would lay a strong foundation for the birth of the much-awaited improvements of the world.

Huxley says that the people must follow the socio-political norms, which is not possible if they do not have a strong personal morality and a sense of commitment and responsibility. The simple example would be to follow the traffic rules strictly and obey other similar public behaviour. Huxley says that the combination of wanting for something novel but preferring only the old ways of doing it is not only self-contradictive but also highly self-destructive. Huxley comes out with the example of driving a car not on road but on the pedestrians, causing innumerable casualties every year, which is equal to a war. He says that following these ideas shall be fundamentally enough to construct a stable and healthy international society.

Aldous Huxley was not only a man of a very sharp intellect, but also of a clear vision. He sensed that rapid industrialization and massive urbanization are going to change man's lifestyle. He comes out with a prediction that the working hours will be reduced to six hours per day, providing a fertile chance for leisure, in the future. Meditating on his contemporary scenario, Huxley is deeply worried about how the leisurely hours are going to be properly utilized by the people. At present, leisure is a privilege for very few people. But in the coming days, with efficient social organization and sophisticated machinery, more and more people will enjoy the fruits of leisure. He cites three authorities namely, Poincare, G. B. Shaw and H. G. Wells, who have concluded that the human beings of the future world would fill their long leisures 'by contemplating the laws of nature'. Different prophets are also hopeful about the proper utilization of leisurely hours. Huxley says:

> Prophets of the future give fundamentally the same answer to this question, with slight variations according to their different tastes. Henri Poincare, for example, imagined that the human beings of the future would fill their long leisures by "contemplating the laws of Nature." Mr. Bernard Shaw is of much the same opinion. Having creased, by the time they are four years old, to take any interest in such childish things as love, art, and the society of their fellow beings, the Ancients in Back to Methuselah devote their indefinitely prolonged existences to meditating on the mysterious and miraculous beauty of the cosmos, Mr. H.G Wells portrays in Men Like Gods a race of athletic chemists and mathematical physicists who go about naked and unlike Mr. Shaw's austerer Ancients, make free

love in a rational manner between the experiments. They also take an interest in the arts and are not above playing games. (AHCE: 411)

But considering the contemporary social scenario and the attitude of the people, Huxley feels disturbed and acutely sorry for the misuse of leisure. James Boswell in his *The Life of Samuel Johnson*, quotes Samuel Johnson, "All intellectual improvement arises from leisure." (219) Huxley talks about the possible ways of the utilization of leisure by the rich and poor. Most of the rich people's preference, Huxley says, is Monte Carlo and Nice, the places notorious for gambling and prostitutes. Huxley calls these places ironically as "an earthly paradise". He says that there are exceptions of those who seek love and an interesting sort of game with them. Some of the people prefer to be engaged with works of charity, politics, local administration and occasionally with scholarly or scientific studies. But it is disgustingly disturbing and morally unacceptable to Huxley that the majority of the population is inclined to Monte Carlo. This concept of leisure of the rich people is not at all encouraging or confidence-giving for the orderly, disciplined and qualitative fabrics of the future international society.

Huxley is not confident that the way the poor people are going to utilise their leisure times productively. Since the people do not have lofty associations and meanings with leisure times in general, they tend to choose activities which are mere killers of times, which is going to retain them in the pathetic conditions, which they already are in. He says that the idea of the poor people on leisure is restricted to looking at cinema, films, reading newspapers, cheap literature, listening to radio, gramophone records, and going from place to place. It is quite unthinkable to Huxley, when he thinks of the possibilities for having prolonged leisure times. He predicts that there would be an enormous increase in amorous lifestyle and time killing. Huxley says:

> If tomorrow or couple of generations, hence, it was made possible for all human   beings to lead the life of leisure which is now led only by a few, the results, so far as I can see, would be as follows: There would be an enormous increase in the demand for such time-killers and substitutes for thought as newspapers, films, fiction, cheap   means of communication, and wireless telephones; to put it in more general terms, there would be an increase in the demand for sport and art. The interest in the fine art of love-making whole be widely extended. And enormous numbers of people, hitherto immune from these mental and moral diseases, would be afflicted by ennui, depression, and universal dissatisfaction. (AHCE: 414)

Huxley is sure that the majority shall devote their leisure to occupations which are utterly stupid, fruitless and even disgusting. He says that there are philosophers, thinkers, educationalists and social reformers who are angry that leisure times are only for those who have nothing to do with lofty thoughts and productive deeds. People who are very intelligent, knowledgeable and try to make their life more meaningful and rich, prefer no sort of cheap entertainment. It would be incorrect to assume that Huxley is against the idea of leisure. He refers to Leo Tolstoy, the great Russian writer, who considered leisure as something 'wicked' and 'absurd'. He thought of leisure lovers as conspirators against the welfare of one's race.

Huxley doesn't consider leisure as a curse. He thinks that in a society where there are intelligent and active minds engaged in mental work, leisure would be 'an unmixed blessing'. Since leisure is apparently connected to mental work, some people may pinpoint the loopholes of educational system and Huxley agrees with them. His observation is that plenty of people who have received the best education, employ their leisure as though they had never been educated at all. Therefore, Huxley believes that if education is made really efficient, contemplating the laws of nature would become the leisure of people.

Aldous Huxley dreams of a world free of all the existing problems of both inside and outside man. Huxley does not an extremist like Tolstoy, when it comes to the idea of leisure. He doesn't impose an outright rejection on the idea of leisure to embrace the concept of work. Huxley's writing style is the evidence that he pays enough respect to

Tolstoy, when he refutes his idea of leisure. This evidently reveals Huxley as not only as a man of intellect, but also a humanistic thinker loaded with many constructive instructions, ideas and pieces of advice to the people of the world to bring in the most wanted changes in them for the betterment of the world peace and the joy of living.

Huxley presents his intense observation, critical opinions and benevolent prescriptions for the entire humanity very convincingly on the canvas of this idea. Huxley's writing style itself, in general, is the indication that he does not want to hurt anyone, since he writes very humorously, when he actually attacks or expresses his moral anger and the tone is so light that any reader can observe that he comes out with sugar-coated expressions for presenting anything bitter and indigestible.

The ethical views of Bertrand Russell

A man without ethics is neither a trustworthy man nor driven by self-respect. Albert Schweitzer, in the book, *Albert Schweitzer: An Anthology*, says, "Ethics is nothing else than reverence for life." (78) Bertrand Russell talks of optimism, not for intellectualizing the idea of optimism, but to reflect the core issues with the optimistic attitude towards anything, which he brilliantly associates with the problematic times he was living in. Russell says that optimism is very pleasantly acceptable, when it is credible and when it is incredible, it causes irritation. There are people who share our troubles with other people and are very optimistic that the problems shall vanish soon. Such people cause so much of emotional disturbance to those who are in trouble, since they do not operate within the limit of the cultural freedom given to them by the person concerned.

Russell says that one has to be extremely careful about being optimistic about other people's troubles and says that in such a situation all that is necessary is the concrete strategy as to what to do in order to quell the problems efficiently or at least to reduce their intensity. He cites the example of a doctor, who is optimistic about curing an ailment, with the prescription of an effective medicine for the ailment and says that a friend, who has the mere words of cheering a person with some disease, is quite an annoyance. Russell says that the optimism of a doctor with a cure is an acceptable optimism unlike a cheering friend's. He says:

The fact is that optimism is pleasant so long as it is credible, but when it is not, it is intensely irritating. Especially irritating is the optimism about our own troubles which is displayed by those who do not have to share them. Optimism about other people's troubles is a very risky business unless it goes with quite concrete proposals as to how to make the troubles disappear or grow less. A medical man has a right to be optimistic about your illness if he can prescribe a treatment which will cure it, but a friend who merely says, 'Oh I expect you will soon feel better', is exasperating. (MO: 70)

Russell says that there were many people, who talked so optimistically about the past two years, but the time span has shown the world all possible negative spectacles. They are like the cheerful friend, who has no moral freedom or right to make any such expression, and not like the medical man, who is a contributor basically and so he hopes his patient to get well soon. A mere cheerfulness has nothing to do with improving the poor condition of those who are starving, Russell says, since he prefers reason to emotion. He says:

Most of the people who have talked optimistically thought the last two years about the bad times have been in the position of the cheerful friend rather than of the medical adviser, and I doubt whether their cheerfulness has added much to the happiness of those who were starving.

In every kind of trouble what is wanted is not emotional cheerfulness but constructive thinking. This fact is gradually being borne in upon the world by the world-wide depression, and in this I perceive the only basis for optimism that our present troubles afford. These troubles can be cured by constructive thinking, not by ballyhoo. (MO:70)

Russell comes out with the prescription that it is only constructive thinking that will safeguard people at their worst times and not being emotional or expecting moral and emotional support from other people. The ultimate distinction between man and animals is man's possession of reasoning capacity and therefore it is no wonder that a humanistic writer like Bertrand Russell propagates the significance of using the head rather than heart even during exigencies, which actually make people have an optimistic approach towards life in general.

Bertrand Russell being a humanist, is against killing human beings in any way, including a person killing himself, suicide. He strongly condemns suicidal tendency and calls it irresponsibility towards life and incapability to withstand the inbuilt challenges of life. Russell, by pointing out certain facts and examples, indirectly attacks the encouragement and justifications that people with suicidal tendency give themselves. Russell is not a philosopher who deals with the subject of suicide merely to intellectualize it to show his knowledge or critical analysis of the subject or a futile philosophizing. His deep humanistic concern that no one should suffer in this world and find life intolerably painful to that extent that the person wants to leave this world. His natural sympathy and mercy towards human ordeals and distress disturbed him to the maximum extent that he made such confessions on private and public platforms.

Russell brings out the anecdote of an Australian farmer, after the country was badly injured in a war, tried to hang himself from a tree but was saved by a neighbour, but the farmer sued a case against the neighbour that he prevented him from escaping the cruel state of his life and inflicted further pain on him. The court understood the condition of the farmer due to the destroyed condition of the country, even though it released the neighbour on some other grounds. A true humanist not only has an interest in the prosperous life of all human beings but also has the capacity and tolerance to listen to the just reasons of the people who has a lot of grievances and complains against life in general. Russell talks about how true are the reasons of the people, who try to commit suicide at the same time comes out with the roaring announcement that it is not only a personal stupidity but also a social negative tendency.

Russell says that attempted suicide is equal to attempted murder in England and America and anyone who tries to commit it on the reason that his or her life is insufferably painful, is imprisoned with the intention of making them love life. Russell says that it is irrational to think that the attempt to kill oneself itself is a crime. The understanding that to kill oneself is equal to killing others seems idiotic to Russell. He gives the example of throwing one's wristwatch into the sea and says that there is a difference between throwing someone's watch and one's own watch into the sea on any ground and to consider them on equal light is not intelligent and logical. He says:

> To say that it is as bad to kill yourself as to kill someone else seems to me absurd. If I take someone else's watch and throw it into the sea, I'm a criminal, but if I throw my own watch into the sea, I am at worst foolish, and if the watch is worthless, I may even be quite sensible. What applies to my watch applies also to my life. When I take another man's life I am taking what does not belong to me, but the question of taking my own life is clearly one that concerns me more than it does anyone else. (MO: 67)

Russell gives a logical justification for suicide, because he believes in the emancipation of original and unhampered thinking and not in any sort of authoritative thrusting of ideas or orders. He believes that through producing clear logical evidence to justify the just reasons behind an action, the doer of the action will understand the logic, which will eventually make him capable of thinking on his own in a logical way about the other side of his deeds, if it is negative and self-destructive. Russell has a deceptive appearance of being an advocate of the suicidal tendency. Russell says that the subject of suicide is to be considered in relation to human sacredness.

Russell talks of different kinds of readers and their purposes behind their act of reading and his humanistic concern that everyone must read to extirpate their ignorance and prejudices to be clear and knowledgeable. He wants to promote a serious type of reading that makes people with strong intellect and original thinking. Russell says that the majority of people does not read and that the majority is not serious about reading but fleeting through pictures. The readers, who know the real taste of the habit of intense reading of all kinds and branches together, make a small number, says Bertrand Russell. Only these people read with the intention of acquiring knowledge and only young people belong to this group. This group reads in order to fly away from all sorts of mental conceits and prejudices, and it is really mature.

Russell says that it is unfortunate that a great number of readers reads to have neither knowledge nor opinions, but for the sheer pleasure of escaping into the world of imagination, avoiding the hard reality of life. He says:

> The majority of mankind red nothing at all; of the remainder, the majority red only the picture papers. Of those who read something more than picture papers, the majority never gets as far as books. All the readers of books – grave and gay, profound and superficial, scientific, literary or lurid – all put together are a very small fraction of the population. Nevertheless, they differ among themselves in all sorts of ways. There are those who read in order to acquire information; they are generally very young. These are those who read in order to acquire confirmation of their prejudices; these people are what is called mature. But the great bulk of readers are seeking neither knowledge nor support for their own opinions, but an escape from reality into the world of imagination. (MO: 65)

This act of escaping from reality to dwell in the world of imagination takes all kinds of forms. Novelettes and films offer the crudest form of slipping into the utopian world for unreal and vicarious pleasures. They are living an unreal world, where an obscure young man or woman achieves splendid success or experience a rich and joyful married life, and this happens at a greater level with those who slip into the history and imagine the abundance and glory of the past ages. A next stage is with the subject of astronomy wherein the aspects of the world of colourful imagination can be found. Russell says that the stars in the book, *Jeans and Eddington*, are very fortunate to lead a quiet and undisturbed life. They are not troubled by the problems of the people in the actual world like the tax collector, the illness of their children and business depression.

Unlike the real life, the life of the characters in the utopian world sooths the readers like the imagination with the stars or nebula. People not only need soothing experience but also excitement. Russell confesses that it is only excitement that prompted his desire for reading. He says that reading detective stories is his most favourite activity. Russell says that detective stories, poetry and astronomy represent different forms of escaping from reality.

He says that according to psychoanalysis the inclination to escape from reality is bad, which Russell partly disagrees with. He says that if imagination makes a person neglect his or her responsibilities, it is destructive and so deplorable, but if it nourishes a person to become constructive, it is highly preferable and appreciable. He says, "The desire to escape from reality becomes a bad thing when it produces delusions or cause a man to neglect his business." (MO: 66) Russell cites some examples. A poor man harassed by his creditors can find a relief, imagining that he is the President of the Bank of France, which is utterly stupid, and the person can be punished for escaping reality. A young woman who forgets herself being into the romantic tale of King Cophetua, neglecting her duty, finally loses her job, also can be punished. But there are other forms of forgetting the real world, fleeing into the world of imagination, which are very much desirable.

Russell actually talks of the role of the power of imagination in making a person be gifted with a creative bent of mind. Mozart, one of the greatest music composers of the world, escaped reality to reach the pleasure dome of creative imagination not to be affected by the worries of his debts, which gifted him with the rarest of music talent and genius. Had Mozart taken the words of the psychoanalysts, he would have been very careful about his balance sheet, but the world would have lost his ever-inspiring symphony. Russell says:

> But there are other forms of escape from reality which are wholly desirable. Mozart used to compose music in order to forget his duns and his debts by escaping into a world of phantasy. If he had followed the advice of eminent psychoanalysts, he would instead have drawn up a careful balance sheet of receipts and expenditures and set to work to devise economies by which the two could be made to balance. If he had

done this, he would have lost his income, and we should have lost his music. Escape from reality, as this instance shows, is not undesirable when it is into a world of imagination recognized as such and used as a means of making reality itself more tolerable. (MO: 66)

Russell says that to escape this reality for the world of imagination to get something very precious with which the hard realities of life can be tolerated and accepted is not deplorable, because such an effort with the world of fancy brings a great boon to the world to soothe 'the fret and fever' of life. Russell says that the most useful inventions would not have been possible without this sort of attempt and so he encourages this sort of reading that ultimately makes readers create something valuable, which they return to the reality with.

The ethical views of Aldous Huxley

Huxley talks about how pleasure-giving it is to collect so much about everything and keep in one's mind to stay updated with all the walks of life in the world and the pleasure of being respected by others, and at the same time, he talks of the pains and unnecessary spirit to stay well aware of the contemporary activities of all the fields. He remembers how passionate he was in being up-to-date with the contemporary literature and other fields, just because the societal expectation that educated and intellectual people must be up-to-date with everything. He says, "Yes, the pleasures of being up-to-date are certainly great. But, then, so are the pleasures of not being up-to-date." (AHCE: 373) Huxley makes a confession that he never was happy and comfortable about whatever he read and did with an intention of being up-to-date.

Huxley says that the people who are into this tedious task of being well-informed of many contemporary things and happenings would think poorly of him for his preference and that the reason why he has chosen the state of not being up-to-date is that he prefers to be himself rather than being fashionable. Huxley says that he has stopped caring for the comments and opinions of others on him, which led to this liberated state. He says:

> These people, it is true, still exist, and will certainly think of the more poorly of me for not being up-to-date, and for admitting the fact. The

reason why I feel that I can afford to be out-of-date is this: I have ceased to care two pins what these people --- the intellectually smart, the leaders or follow-my-leaders of metal fashion --- think of me, or indeed of anything else under the sun. To find it more agreeable to be, not fashionable, but myself." (AHCE: 374)

Huxley says that he remembers with the depth of his aloneness how foolish he was in wasting his time to be up-to-date, because he yearned for the appreciation of others in staying fashionable. Huxley says that he remembers reading the book Ulysses, attended many theatres for drams and went to many music concerts, which he deeply regrets because he thinks that he wasted an uncountable valuable hours spent on them. He says:

> When, from the depths of my calm solitude, I reflect on the many extraordinarily foolish and time-wasting things I have done for the sake of being up-to-date and earning the approval of the fashionable, I shudder and am amazed that I could ever have been so idiotic. Thus, I remember spending at least seventy-two precious now irremediably perished hours in reading Mr. James Joyce's Ulysses. I remember passing hundreds of evenings at the first

nights of the most boring plays (though it is true I was paid for doing so). I remember listening to the whole concerts of music by Mr.Gustav Holst. I remember passing whole afternoons among the landscapes of K.Marchand and his English followers. And for what? To whom is the benefit, as we used to ask in Latin? Merely that I might be able to say that I had read the portentous and boring book, heard the dim music, seen the plays, and thrilled aesthetically before the significance of those painted forms. (AHCE: 374-375)

Huxley says that he is as happy as when he was fashionable now even without that socially supreme status of being up-to-date. He says that he is no more interested in what the intelligentsia of the world has thought about, written or spoken recently and that the distance between himself and the contemporary civilization is the inexhaustible source of serenity, peace and areal happiness in his life. He says, "But now, I find that it really does not matter in that least what the mentally smart think. I find that I am quite happy in out-of-dateness; what is more, I find that I don't miss much. The distance at which I live from contemporary civilization acts, as it were, as a filter." (AHCE: 375)

Huxley talks about the necessity of extricating from the claws of the socially imposed importance of knowing the novelties, which gifts one's leisure and calmness with rich material to meditate on for personal enrichment. Real work starts only after leaving this societal expectation and anxiety that one has to be accepted by those who are truly regarded to be great intellectually. Such a liberation leaves a person at the freedom to think, talk to the people one truly loves and read the books that were in the list to be read, when there is sufficient time. Huxley says that these activities are the principal joys and advantages of not being up-to-date. He says:

> To be free from the socially imposed necessity of knowing about novelties is to endow oneself with leisure and calm. It enables one to work; it leaves one at liberty to think --- a process which, like almost everyone else, I used to detest, preferring to occupy my mind with the various substitutes for thought, from newspapers to the Freudian interpretation of dreams, which modern civilization provides in ever-increasing quantities for the relief of mind-haunted humanity. It leaves one at liberty, I repeat, to think (and once one is used to it, the activity is really quite agreeable); it gives one time and inclination to talk with the few people one likes, about interesting things; and excuses one from having to talk with the causally

met many, about the things which one finds boring. It creates the leisure to read the books one always meant and wanted, but never had the time, to read, owing to the press of new noels, plays, and the like, a knowledge of which is essential, if one is to sustain a conversation is polite and intellectual smart society. These are the principal joy and advantages of not being up-to-date; and very considerable I find them. (AHCE: 375)

Huxley is not happy about the models offered by the world of intellect and so he comes forward courageously as to inform the world that people must know what to do to lead a healthy life, mentally, emotionally and intellectually. They should not take wrong models and expectations from the society that they deem to be superior to them. He announces to the world that original thinking is more important than trying to keep many unwanted information just because the world of fashionable society exposes it to be superior and distinct. Huxley, being a humanist and an intellectual, aims at bringing clarity to the people on the unnecessary weight that they carry pleasurably, without which they shall lead a fee and comfortable life.

Huxley wants to talk to the people of the world about the mentality to taste pleasures in the modern times. He says that the world has seen many dangers to the civilization. The first to be encountered was the militarism of Prussia and then the German military moves and the two famous wars that took place quite unexpectedly for a very long time. Huxley includes the French militarism. He says:

> WE HAVE HEARD a great deal, since 1914, about the things which are a menace to civilization. First it was Prussian militarism; then the Germans at large; then the prolongation of the war; then the shortening of the same; then, after a time, the Treaty of Versailles; then French militarism – with, all the while, a running accompaniment of such minor menaces as Prohibition, Lord Northcliffe, Mr.Bryan, Comstockery. (AHCE: 354)

Huxley says that the world civilization was strong enough to withstand the menacing combined attacks of all these enemies admirably well. He says that the dangers that confronts our civilization at present are not the external dangers like men driven by devastating anger, horrible impending war, and the potential possibility of becoming impecunious that wars inflict on the people of the world, leaving them to become uncivilized as to cruelly fight among themselves for mere survival. The most devastative dangers that cruelly keeps the worthy lives of the people of world under a horrendous state are the dangers that dwell within man. They are the potential threat for the courageous mind of human beings to thrive well in life. He says, "No the dangers which confront our civilization are not so much the eternal dangers --- wild men, wars, and the bankruptcy that wars bring after them. The most alarming dangers are those which menace it from within, that threaten the mind rather than the body and estate of contemporary man." (AHCE: 324-355)

Huxley here indirectly teaches the people of the world that it is not the body or the tangible asserts that one amasses which are the most important in life, but the mind, affecting of which, is affecting the vey life of the person concerned. This indirect message is not only philosophical but also spiritual that talks of the most prominent truth about life itself, because modern people are misguided that happiness lies in earning money and leading an incomparably lavish and rich practical life.

Huxley says that pleasure is the most dangerous poison by a process of auto-intoxication that the modern civilization brews within its own bowels. Here Huxley does not talk about all kinds of pleasure, but the intentionally organized pleasure in order to distract the people of the world to execute the command of the top level government officials and rulers. The organized criminal offence of making people believe that real personal and social pleasures lie only in doing a particular activity, associated with a particular organization and not in any other. The typical example is that the attitude of the people that being a government officer and working very hard for hours together are considered a superior status and a supreme pleasure when compared with being very creative about writing on something interesting to let out one's passion for intellectual freedom, tasting the unique feel of being an author and a critic and feeling a range of freedom that the majority has nothing to do with. He says:

> Of all the various poisons which modern civilization, by a process of auto intoxication, brews quietly up within its own bowels, few, it seems to me, are more deadly (while none appears more harmless) than that curious and appalling thing that is technically known as "pleasure". "Pleasure" (I place the world between inverted commas to show that I mean, not real pleasure, but the organized activities officially known by the same name) "pleasure" --- what nightmare visions the word evokes! Like every man of sense and good feeling, I abominate work. But I would rather put in eight hours a day at a Government office than be condemned to lead a life of "pleasure"; I would even, I believe, prefer to write a million words of journalism a year. (AHCE: 355)

Aldous Huxley says that the man of the past was more logical and courageous than the present man. Their conclusions and decisions through the method of arguments and meditations can be said to be idiotic, but their capacity to be determined about taking a decision or to act in a way as they thought of were stronger than how a modern man makes decisions about something in his life. They believed in their flawless arguments and the cause for which they had to take certain decision, which were well-executed, thanks to their decisive personality. Huxley talks of Wesley, who believed in witchcraft, because he believed in the Bible that talks of witchcraft. So, it is believed that witchcraft is true, based on the statement or belief that the Bible is true. Losing belief in witchcraft is losing faith in the Bible. Huxley sys:

> Our fathers were more logical than we, and more courageous. The conclusions to which their arguments led them might be manifestly idiotic or immoral; but that did not prevent them, once they were convinced that the premises were sound and the argument flawless, from drawing those conclusions and, if necessary, acting on them. starting from the premises that everything in the Bible is literally true, Wesley was necessarily led to believe in witchcraft. The Bible is true; witchcraft is mentioned in the Bible as existing; therefore, witchcraft exists. The argument is unimpeachable. In the century of Hume and Voltaire,

Wesley believed in witches. If you abandon belief in witchcraft, he insisted, you abandon belief in the Bible. He was logical and had the courage of his opinions. (AHCE: 394-395)

Huxley says that he does not agree with the logic or argument of Wesley, but he appreciates the courage to do it and his intellectual honesty. Unlike, the man of the past, the modern man is afraid to take any decision and the reasons, logic and the ideas for the construction of the intentions behind taking a decision do not have any strong impact on his mind and so he is doubtful about the trustworthiness and the possibility of getting success out of following them. Modern man commits the basic mistake of being with so much of compromise, but with too little logical consistency. Huxley's humanistic voice here is on the indecisive nature of the modern man, which is fundamentally self-destructive. He says:

> I do not happen to agree with Wesley; but I admire his spirit and his intellectual honesty. There is too much compromise, nowadays and too little logical consistency. We are afraid of drawing the logical conclusions from the premises in which we profess to believe. We do not like to make any very definite or sweeping assertion for fear that by so doing we might be making fools of

ourselves. The manifest contradictions which exist between different sections of our beliefs, between our beliefs and our actions, we vaguely harmonize, if we try to harmonize them at all, in some dim Higher Synthesis, where black is the same as white, good as evil and nonsense as sense. (AHCE: 395)

Huxley talks against the famous socio-political ideology or statement that all men are equal in democracy and he says that this is true only in mystic sense and not in any political or social sense. Men are all equal in being the children of God and in the capacity to suffer, love and distinguish good from evil. Men are equal only in those capacities, but not in their capacity to fight to govern others or themselves. Huxley says that to believe that all are equal is the fundamental idiotic mistake of democracy and people are made believe through such cunning propagations for the political and economic benefits of rulers, aristocrats and other powerful people of a democratic country. Huxley says:

Democracy is based on assuming that all men are equal. Now that assumption is true, but only in a mystical sense. Men are equal as being all the children of God – as being all endowed with a capacity for suffering, loving, and knowing good and evil. They are not equal in any of

> those abilities which make men fit to govern themselves or others. The mistake of the democrats has been to suppose that men are equal in every way and to base practical politics on this gratuitous and false assumption. (AHCE: 397)

Huxley says that the idea that all are equal in democracy is not something unimportant and glorifies the true significance of having such a statement that has a huge impact in the minds of all citizens of all democratic countries, in spite of having no tangible evidence to support that statement practically. He says that equality in democracy, the cradle of the idea of 'humanitarianism', is the concept that deeply modified the society. Huxley says that the defenders of humanitarianism are the supporters of the belief that all are equal in democracy. Even the rich people in a democratic society admit that even the poor people of the society have the same rights and freedom and serve the poor considerably either directly or indirectly. Huxley's humanitarianism is predominantly exposed here, when he talks of the merits of humanitarianism, which has a very strong connection with the benevolent belief that all are equal in democracy. Even though he talks of the lack of humanitarianism in the world, he does not fail to admit the bright side of the belief. He says:

> It must not be supposed that, simply because the idea of the equality of man is mystical, it is therefore

unimportant. On the contrary, it is one of the highest significance. It is an idea which has already profoundly modified future. Humanitarianism is the expression of that idea. We are all humanitarians now, whatever our political opinions and whatever our social position. Even those who are in possession of wealth and power admit that those who possess nothing have certain rights. They are perpetually giving away little bits of their wealth and power to be dispossessed. (AHCE: 397)

Huxley wants to compare the productive impacts of the belief that all are equal in democracy and the destructive consequences of the lack of such an impact under the rule of a tyrant. Unlike the people, who have the freedom and possibilities of getting their basic needs, at least, in a democratic country, in a tyrannical country, people are handicapped by poverty, regrettable conditions and insufficient education that lead them not towards the higher pursuits of life, due to its absence. Huxley says that the paupers and sufferers of a country due to its indifference to equality must be helped by humanitarianism and be enriched so that their life will be improved, giving an unshakable hope for such people to get out the wretched condition for a healthy and comfortable life. Huxley says:

> In tyrannical society, where humanitarian principles are not recognized, nine-tenths of the individuals composing that society are so unfairly handicapped by poverty, bad conditions, and inadequacy of education that they are not in a position to compete for any of the higher prizes of life. By ameliorating the lot of the dispossessed, humanitarianism removes this handicap, and thus, by multiplying the competitors, tends to create an intenser and therefore biologically more stimulating competition. (AHCE: 398)

Huxley motivates that there must be a sense of competition among the people of a country so that all will strive to become well in life, exhibiting their special capacity and talents so that the country shall have the bright chance of having many able people for the most important governmental activities, which is the actual political justification of humanitarianism. Huxley says that such a spirit for competition eventually increases the number of efficient people for the leadership of a country. He says, "Humanitarianism, then, has a biological function --- to render possible an intenser competition within society. When all men are free to compete and all start equal, the chance of getting able men at the head of affairs is obviously increased. That is the political justification of humanitarianism. Society should be run on humanitarian principles because an increase in the number of competitors increase the chances of efficient leadership." (AHCE: 398) Huxley says that human beings must be changed to bring in humanitarianism to the society and the world ultimately. With the collective change, through a healthy competitive spirit to be highly productive and contributing to the society, the long-awaited glorious societal change can be achieved.

The educational views of Bertrand Russell

Bertrand Russell talks of the purpose of education, the present condition of education, the responsibilities of a teacher, the present lamentable condition of teachers, the responsibilities of students and what should be done to resolve the existing problems in the field of education. Russell's humanistic observations and recommendations to resolve the problems of the field of education and improve its standard are very significant. He says that the role of education in forming and shaping the character of children and their opinions is admirably powerful. Russell says that education is a powerful force that stands for fundamental changes in the world. He says that education makes children think originally and does not make them think like their teachers. Bertrand Russell says that education does not make children merely choose a political party to be a member of it, but enables them to choose intelligently between parties. He says:

Education would not aim at making them belong to this party or that, but at enabling them to choose intelligently between the parties: it would aim at making them able to think, not at making them think what their teachers think. Education as a political weapon could not exist if we respected the rights of children. If we respected the rights of children, we should educate them so as to give them the knowledge and the mental habits required for forming independent opinions; but education as political institution endeavours to form habits and to circumscribe knowledge in such a way as to make one set of opinions inevitable. (BWBR: 380)

He says that it makes children think originally and does not make them think like their teachers. He says that if it is true that we respect the important fundamental rights of children, we must educate them as to make them become knowledgeable and cultivate the habit of constructing independent opinions so that education as a political weapon shall perish. But a political institution wants to instil a set of opinions to be respected and followed without any question. Russell says that the two great principles of Justice and Liberty, which play a vital role in the construction of the society, are not enough in the field of education. Education must essentially impart many useful ideas on what makes a good life. He says that the teachers do not have freedom to be the guardians and mentors of the children at their own sought-after freedom and desire. Authority in education is understandably unavoidable, but Russell says that it must not go to the extent of damaging liberty, which is the soul of educating children. Russell talks of showing respect and cultivating the nobility of respecting others.

Russell goes on to reflect the present condition of the field of education, including the plight of teachers due to the workload that they straddle with. He says that the rules to be followed come from the government to the field of education. Teachers struggle with their large classes, fixed and stagnant curriculum and overwork and they can only produce students with mediocrity, without any reverence for the child. He says that such a reverence is possible only with imagination and affection that they are foolish, tender, weak, tender children, who are yet to learn, implement and achieve and that the teachers are strong and wise. If this is not the attitude, the teachers will have an indifference and contempt for the children for their inferior status of being beginners. He says:

> In education, with its codes of rules emanating from a government office, its large classes and fixed curriculum and overworked teachers, its determination to produce a dead level of glib mediocrity, the lack of reverence for the child is all but universal. Reverence requires imagination in respect of those who have least actual achievement or power. The child is weak and superficially foolish, the teacher is strong, and in an everyday sense wiser than the child. The teacher without reverence, or the bureaucrat without reverence, easily despises the child for these outward inferiorities. He thinks it is his duty to 'mould' the child: in imagination he is the potter with the clay. And so he gives to the child some unnatural shape, which hardens with age, producing strains and spiritual dissatisfaction, out of which grow cruelty and envy, and the belief that others must be compelled to undergo the same distortions. (BWBR: 380-381)

Russell says that reverence to children does not come out of a sense of duty to shape them, but it feels itself in all living creatures. A true reverence is natural and does its activity of educating, shaping and launching them towards the pursuit of their goals that they have formed for themselves. He says that children are sacred, tough to define, vast, unadulterated purity and individuality and very precious, the growing principle of life. A teacher with real reverence for the children feels accountable with humility that exhibits something noble that is not synonymous with the self-confidence of teachers and parents. Such an accountable person knows that they are superficially weak, dependent and helpless and becomes rally trustworthy to the children, and he will have imaginations about the growth and strength of the children and their accomplishments and powerful positions in future, by means of excavating their strength and potency. He says:

> The man who has reverence will not think it is his duty to 'mould' the young. He feels in all that lives, but especially in human beings, and most of all in children, something sacred, indefinable, unlimited, something individual and strangely precious, the growing principle of life, an embodied fragment of the dumb striving of the world. In the presence of a child, he feels an unaccountable humility --- a humility not easily defensible on a rational ground, and yet somehow nearer to wisdom than the easy

self-confidence of many parents and teachers. (BWBR: 383)

The teacher will have such dreams about the children and will be longing to help them win the battles of their aspirations. He will do it not for satisfying any institutional expectations or authority but to help the children explore their potentiality and operate at its height and experience the fulfilment of self-actualizing and reaching inspiring heights in their life. Russell says that only such a concerned teacher will be omnipotent and heroic to his authority, without invading the actual principles of liberty about educating children. He says:

> The outward helplessness of the child and the appeal of dependence make him conscious of the responsibility of a trust. His imagination shows him what the child may become, for good or evil, how its impulses many be developed or thwarted, how its hopes must be dimmed and the life in it grow less living, how its trust will be bruised and its quick desires replaced by brooding will. All this gives him a longing to help the child in its own battle; he would equip and strengthen it, not for some outside end proposed by the State or by any other impersonal authority, but for the ends which the child's own spirit is obscurely seeking. The man who feels this can wield the authority of an educator without infringing the principle of liberty. (BWBR: 381)

In the modern education system, the focus is on the capacity of students to amass material wealth and reach lucrative positions, which ultimately make them very ordinary. He says that almost all educational systems have a political motive, the aim of which is to support and strengthen some national, religious and social group, competing with other groups. This competitive spirit to be superior to the other groups that decides which subject should be taught, the knowledge to be imparted and the knowledge to be hidden from them, including the intellectual and mental habits that these students have to attain and follow throughout their life, as a result, this system does not do anything to nourish the internal growth of the mind and spirit of the pathetic pupils. Russell says that the more a person is educated, the less is the impulse for original thinking to be decisive and creative in life and they live with the mechanical aptitude taught in schools and colleges.

Russell emphasizes on education for all and says that the world needs very talented doctors, advocates and engineers and wants the student's community, when they aspire for higher education, to be careful about their preference for a branch of study and its compatibility with their personality and personal and professional goals. He says, "All children must continue to be taught how to read and write, and some must continue to acquire the knowledge needed for such professions as medicine or law or engineering. The higher education required for the sciences and the arts is necessary for those to whom it is suited." (BWBR: 382)

Russell says that the subject of history is the most controversial, since it is taught in all countries to exaggerate their bright side to give an impression to their citizens that their country is the best in all possible ways, hence superior to the rest.

Children learn to believe that their country has never been truly defeated by any country and those who attacked their country are unrefined and the most dangerous people in the world and this impression becomes inseparable from their mind. Russell says:

> History, in every country, is so taught as to magnify that country: children learn to believe that their own country has always been in the right and almost always victorious, that it has produced almost all the great men, and that it is in all respects superior to all other countries. Since these beliefs are flattering, they are easily absorbed, and hardly ever dislodged from instinct by later knowledge. (BWBR: 382)

Russel impliedly says that the foolish pride of man eclipses certain truths about a country, preventing its citizens to know the actual history of their country, giving them the impression that they are the best in the world, which psychologically distance them from others. This impression is the fundamental reason to become eternally prejudiced on people, culture and religion.

Russell says that education must bolster the instinct and desire for truth and not for creating the conviction that a particular creed is the truth.

Russell says that inactive children with mere beliefs become prejudiced, cynical, intellectually hopeless and they become hyper-critical about everything to make all look foolish, being unable to be operated by any creative impulse, thereby destructing it in others. He says that a strong rational attitude is the only virtue to escape from this misleading forces. He says, "In those whose minds are not very active the result is the omnipotence of prejudice; whole the few whose thought cannot be wholly killed become cynical, intellectually hopeless, destructively critical, able to make all that is living seem foolish, unable themselves to supply the creative impulses which they destroy in others." (BWBR: 384) It is advocated that free and creative intellectual enquiries must be cultivated to be with clarity and truth about anything.

Education is conceptualized as a drill to achieve unanimity through slavishness and is convincingly stated that it is the path to victory and prosperity. There are many important practical affairs that require the power of human intellect and intelligence and not inactivity. Russell says that education that produces gullibility in children brings them to the stages of mental decay very quickly and that at least, a minimum of indispensable development can be achieved only through a spirit for free enquiry. He says, "And in the modern world so much intellect is required in practical affairs that even the external victory is more likely to be won by intelligence than by docility. Education in credulity leads by quick stages to mental decay; it is only by keeping alive the spirit of free inquiry that the indispensable minimum of progress can be achieved." (BWBR: 384) The slavishness and gullibility vanish with the true light of education, an unbridled, fresh and liberated state of mind for rational rumination on anything.

Russell says that certain mental habits like obedience and discipline, being ruthless for worldly success, acceptance to the wisdom of the teachers without any question are instilled in the minds of students by the teachers and the educational system, which is against life itself. Independence and impulse are more important than obedience and discipline and the ethics of education is that it should show the seeds of justice in the minds of students. Contempt should be replaced with reverence and the capacity to understand the ideas and opinions of others. It should stop forcing children to embrace credulity and encourage them to doubt constructively. The education which is wanted presently must cultivate the love for mental adventure and being bold in thoughts. Getting satisfaction out of reaching a status and feeling superior about having subordinates are the immediate evil effects of an undesirable system of education, which promotes only acquiring material power and richness. He says:

> Certain mental habits are commonly instilled by those who are engaged in educating: obedience and discipline, ruthlessness in the struggle for worldly success. Contempt towards opposing groups, and an unquestioning credulity, a passive

acceptance of the teacher's wisdom. All these habits are against life. Instead of obedience and discipline, we ought to aim at preserving independence and impulse. Instead of ruthlessness, education should try to develop justice in thought. Instead of contempt, it ought to instil reverence, and the attempt at understanding; towards the opinions of others, it ought to produce, not necessarily acquiescence, but only such opposition as is combined with imaginative apprehension and a clear realization of the grounds for opposition. Instead of credulity, the object should be to stimulate constructive doubt, the love of mental adventure, the sense of worlds to conquer by enterprise and boldness in thought. (BWBR: 384)

Russell says that obedience and discipline are important and indispensable when there is an order to be maintained or instruction is to be given to a class, but when compared with the ulterior motive of the system of education to produce only obedient servants to obey orders without letting them to think on their own, the significance of obedience and discipline in the class is to be rethought of. Obedience, according to Russell, is yielding one's will to an outside direction and it is the counterpart of authority and blind obedience to authority hampers the natural growth and function of the intellect of the children.

Russell talks of the plight of teachers also by their authority. He says that the authority thinks that the teachers can work like bank clerks for hours, which will produce intense lassitude and lack of interest out of irritation of nerves and shall eventually be mechanical in their speaking and activities with the children. Teachers should be given enough freedom to have natural love for teaching. Russell talks of how teachers should be and function with children, while teaching them. He says that a class, having children small in number is highly preferable, which is compatible with not only pleasurable teaching but also the feasibility to have an eclectic teaching methods. Russell says that teachers should not think of dealing with as many ideas as possible in a day. They should think of teaching a subject and the extent to which it can be taught should be under consideration according to the mental needs of the students in the class. This leads to a friendly relationship between teachers and students instead of hostility, which actually extirpates the misunderstanding that education does take away their pleasurable time and joy. He says:

> A teacher out to have only as much teaching as can be done, on most days, with actual pleasure in the work, and with an awareness of the pupil's mental needs. The result would be a relation of friendliness instead of hostility between teacher and pupil,   a realization on the part of most pupils that education serves to develop their own lives and is not merely an outside imposition,

interfering with play and demanding many hours of sitting still. (BWBR: 385)

Russell says that the kind of discipline desirable is that which comes from within, which one acquires through the power of devoting consistent attention and endeavour, experiencing many sufferings and ordeals in the intellectual task. This task involves submitting minor impulses to Will, which is directed by the conflagration of a creative desire, without which accomplishing a serious ambition is not possible. This necessary discipline is out a strong desire for the end and not out of anything immediately attainable and a true education must nourish such desires. Russell says that it is one's will that begets such a desire and not any outside authority and that this does not happen with the presently existing system of education. He says:

> The desirable kind of discipline is the kind that comes from within, which consists in the power of pursuing a distant object steadily, forgoing and suffering many things on the way. This involves the subordination of minor impulses to will, the power of a directing action by large creative desires even at moments when they are not vividly alive. Without this, no serious ambition, good or bad, can be realized, no consistent purpose can dominate. This kind of discipline is very necessary but can only result from strong desires for ends not immediately attainable, and can only be

produced by education if education fosters such desires, which it seldom does at present. Such discipline springs from one's own will, not from outside authority. It is not this kind which is sought in most schools, and it is not this kind which seems to me an evil. (BEBR: 386)

Russell says that the true success of the traditional higher education is to produce mental discipline and that it can't be achieved through compulsion. Russell talks of the nature of children and the way they prefer to learn their subjects. He says that children are spontaneous and enjoy acquiring knowledge only spontaneously and they do not want to learn anything that they do not desire to learn and that this is the best method of education according to him. He says, "The child's attention is wholly spontaneous, as in play; it enjoys acquiring knowledge in this way and does not acquire any knowledge which it does not desire. I am convinced that this is the nest method of education with young children: the actual results make it almost impossible to think otherwise." (BEBR: 386) Russell talks of the importance of giving prolonged attention to something and says that it is not found naturally but acquired through outside force. He says that some children, who have enough intellectual desires, do have the capacity for devoting their attention continuously in learning something, through exercising their free will. For others an external inducement is a must to make them learn something entirely.

Russell says that children are afraid of receiving official commands about taking great efforts in their fields and that should be done through stimulating advice and not through forcing them to use their potential. A good teacher does it to any student of a remarkable mental capacity, who is capable of great achievements. Russell says that to enrich the mental capacity of students to achieve many things, education, attained through books, is not the best method and that teachers are to be strictly informed that they must succeed in this method of capacitating the students to become achievers. If not it is easy for teachers to be sluggish and blame their children for not functioning efficiently, when the fault is actually with them. Here Russell talks of talking to the students as mentors and not as mere traditional teachers, associated only with the act of mechanical teaching. He says:

> A good teacher ought to be able to do this for any boy who is capable of much mental achievement; and for many of the others the present purely bookish education is probably not the best. In this way, so long as the importance of mental discipline is realized, it can probably be attained, whenever it is attainable, by appealing to the pupil's consciousness of his own needs. So long as teachers are not expected to succeed by this method, it is easy for them to slip into a slothful dullness and blame their pupils when the fault is really their own. (BWBR: 387)

Russell is against the act of advertising the successes of pupils and says that a negative competitive spirit is watered by the act. Russell is very deep about his comment that it actually encourages competitive spirit that comes to be in the forefront of the decision taken in all spears of life, including socio-political areas. Instead of nurturing the competitive spirit, Russell says that the latent inclination for knowledge in young children has to be nourished. The talented minds of children, in being competitive, learn certain ideas and concept by heart, which are very disinterestedly supervised and examined by the teachers for the purpose of awarding diplomas and degrees.

Russell condemns this system stating that it is, for the abler students, nothing but a long tiresome task of giving and receiving examination tips and textbook facts because there is no time for the indulgence in intellectual taste. The most intelligent students are ultimately disgusted with their learning, which they try to forget to get into a life of useful actions and these children also get into the trap of running for money, which seriously affects their spontaneous desires in life. He says:

> For the abler boys there is no time for thought, no time for the indulgence of intellectual taste, from the moment of first going to school until the moment of leaving the university. From first to last there is nothing but one long drudgery of examination tips and textbook facts. The most intelligent, at the end, are disgusted

with learning, longing only to forget it and to escape into a life of action. Yet there, as before, the economic machine holds them prisoners and all their spontaneous desires are bruised and thwarted. (BWBR: 387)

Russell says that the examination system makes the children think of knowledge from a utilitarian point of view that it is a road to money-making and not the truth that it is a gateway to wisdom. The examination system affects those who have a strong intellectual interest and so they feel the pressure of being compelled to prepare for mere examinations. Russell says that almost all children consider education as a means to attain the status of being superior to others. This system is corrupted and putrefied with ruthlessness and social inequality. Inequality is contrary to justice and those who succeed are benefited by it.

Russell says that accepting the wisdom of a teacher passively does not take independent thought and looks deceptively rational because of the belief that the teacher knows whatever he teaches more than his pupils. This passive acceptance is a way to get into the good books of the teachers also. Russell talks of how dangerous passive acceptance is. He says that students of passive acceptance cannot become leaders, and they will be in search of leaders, instead of taking the position of a leaser, since they have been accustomed to being only followers. Russell says that this is want is found with Churches, Governments, party caucuses and all the other organizations, where these types of people are supporters of the old system, which are detrimental to the nation and even themselves. He says that there cannot be any room for independence of thoughts, even though promoting this is a part of an educational system. So the students must be given the freedom of thinking and articulating their opinion freely through conducting various activities that necessitates critical thinking and being expressive, connecting with others. He says:

> Passive acceptance of the teacher's wisdom is easy to most boys and girls. It involves no effort of independent thought and seems rational because the teacher knows more than his pupils; it is moreover the way to win the favour of the teacher unless he is a very exceptional man. Yet the habit of passive acceptance is a disastrous one in later life. It causes men to seek a leader, and to accept as a leader whoever is established in that position. It makes the power of Churches, Governments, party caucuses, and all the other organizations by which plain men are misled into supporting old systems which are harmful to the nation and to themselves. It is possible that there would not be much independence of thought even if education did everything to promote it; but there would certainly be more than there is at present. If the object were to make pupils think, rather than to make them accept certain conclusions, education would be conducted quite differently: there would

be less rapidity of instruction and more discussion, more occasions when pupils are encouraged to express themselves, more attempt to make education concern itself with matters in which the pupils feel some interest. (BEBR: 388)

Russell says that the power of original thinking comes to a person who has travelled beyond the daily routines of the mundane life and from the practical life's triviality and wearisomeness, breaking down the prison walls of the commonplace. Russell says that the pleasure and the supremacy of creative thoughts and original criticism are not known to the majority in the world. He says that the power of the world of creative thinking is an incomparable adventurous spirit, which men can experience instead of welcoming war to show their thirst for adventurous activities, since creative thinking has nothing to do with cruel thinking, blood-shed and destroying our own species, but increases one's self-worth and dignity and brings peace of mind as a result of creative splendour, due to which the education of the mind is be valued so high. He says:

The powers of thought, the vast regions which it can master, the much vaster regions which it can only dimly suggest to imagination, given to those whose minds have travelled beyond the daily round an amazing richness of material, an escape from the trivial and wearisomeness of familiar routine, by which the whole of life is filled with interest, and the prison walls of the commonplace are broken down. The same love of adventure which takes men to the South Pole, the same passion for a conclusive trial of strength which leads some men to welcome war, can find in creative thought an outlet which is neither wasteful nor cruel, but increases the dignity of man by incarnating in life some of the shining splendour which the human spirit is bringing down out of the unknown. To give this joy, in a greater or less measure, to all who are capable of it, is the supreme end for which the education of the mind is to be valued. (BWBR: 388)

Russell says that it is the young people in the world who know the joy of mental adventure when compared with the grown-up people. A natural spirit for mental adventure is quite common in children and it grows rampantly out of living in the world of imagination and creative thinking, but it education in their later life kills it. Russell says, "The joy of mental adventure is far commoner in the young than in grown men and women. Among children it is very common and grows naturally out of the period of make-believe and fancy. It is rare in later life because everything is done to kill it during education." (BWBR: 389) He says that there is nothing in the world like fear that every man is afraid of, which is more than their fear for devastation in generation and even death.

Russell aims at refining human mind and psychology through creative thinking to become rational beings with the right kind of education. He talks of the nature of fear and how men are afraid of many things, especially to think on various concepts that they follow so as to have their opinions. He says that an institution inspired by fear cannot give us hope for life. Hope is the creative principle of human activities, he says. It is only the spirit of safeguarding anything good that has made man great and modern education is not inspired by hope and so does not achieve great results, since careful desire to preserve the past than the hope of creating future is the dominating force of the administrators of the field of teaching.

Russell says that the purpose of education is not to be teemed with dead facts, but to create. It should be out of inspiration and not like the wish to restore the old and shimmering beauty of something valuable after it has vanished. He is optimistic and has a vision that in the future, the world of creative thoughts will dominate and become the ruler of the world and says that those who are taught with the aim of creating such personalities, shall be with the true essence of life. They will be suffused with hope and joy and become great contributors to the unshakable faith in the glory that human endeavours can create in this world.

Russell discusses what is naturally suitable for men and women to excel in the selected branch of study or interest. Russell says that it is utterly stupid and highly piteous to impose the kind of education that has made men worthless on women in the name of enriching them. The education that is mostly masculine does not have anything to do with arousing feminine interest. Russell makes a fundamental difference between men and women and says that the true emancipation of women is not in the mere influence that they have to become like men. Men have certain natural traits and interests, which they develop through their education and self-interested activities and the same is applicable with women, if they are to achieve true emancipation as women. He says:

> As regards intelligence, the attempts to ignore native differences are beginning to seem a mistake. A great deal of the scholastic education of men is worthless, and it is a pity to inflict it on women. The most important part of men's education is the most masculine, namely, that concerned with science and machinery, and it is this part especially which almost always fails to arouse feminine interest. (MO: 75)

Russell says that it is insane to think and conclude that female intelligence is inferior to masculine intelligence. Men have set a standard of intelligence and made it very suitable for themselves and created a mechanical civilization, which does not have any room for human values. Even if women had been left to the freedom of being themselves, they would have never invented machines. If they had been asked to contribute effectively for human civilization, they would not have forgotten to preserve human values, shinning mechanical ingenuity totally. He says:

> It would be foolish to draw the inference that female intelligence is inferior to that of the male. Men have set a standard of intelligence and have instinctively set it to suit themselves; they have created a mechanical civilization which largely ignores human values. Women left to themselves would, I believe, never have invented machines. But if they had been able freely to contribute to the sum total of civilization, they would not have forgotten to preserve what is valuable in human life and would not have been led astray, as men have been, by a blind worship of mechanical ingenuity. (MO: 76)

Russell announces that the real contribution that the true characteristic qualities of women could make, have not been made so far, because of lack of freedom for women. Since women have been receiving the education compatible with men, their prudence to acquire what is suitable for them to make substantial and the most productive contributions has been debarred. Russell comes out with a humanistic and optimistic note that this condition will soon disappear to see women to reach their true empowerment. He says:

> Contribution which women's nature would enable them to make, they have not yet been able to make, because they have not been free. They have been exposed to an

education designed for men, and they have been debarred by prudery from the kind of education which would have most developed their faculties. This state of affairs, however, is rapidly improving, and I think we may hope that before many decades have passed women will be in a position to be no longer either restrictive or imitative but genuinely creative in important ways for which their faculties are more adapted than those of men. (MO: 76)

The educational views of Aldous Huxley

The concept of education of Aldous Huxley is based on the understanding of the inter-connection among knowledge, rationality and human psychology. Huxley says that rational thought is still not possible without knowledge and that human beings know very little about psychology, heredity and the relationship between mind and body. Education is nothing but applied psychology and heredity and applied psycho-physiology and says that because of these reasons, rational thinking in the field of education has been distanced. Being knowledgeable about the subject of biological inheritance and the relation between the mind and body is the proper way of meditating on the concept of education, since it is about observational capacity, associating skills in the process of learning and digesting ability to be confident about one's intense knowledge and understanding on a subject. It is not a wonder that Huxley has such a stupendous approach to the concept of education, because he is basically a university professor. Huxley says:

> Rational foresight is impossible without knowledge, and we still know relatively very little bout psychology, or heredity, or the relations of mind and body. By education is simply applied psychology, applied heredity and applied psycho-physiology. It follows therefore that rational foresight is still, to a great extent, impossible in the sphere of education. (BW: 133)

Huxley says that every professor must foresee the child's future development. A teacher or a professor must observe so as to discover the latent talent of a child to be polished and then only, the activities and assignments related to the learning will not only be effortless but also passionate for the children. He says that a teacher should observe what is a child good at and probably what sort of place the child can occupy in the society in terms of power and efficiency and accordingly training has to be given to the particular child. Huxley says that this is the only strategy to make our educational system very effective. Huxley quotes Mr. J.B.S. Haldane to say that the combined efforts of the experts of the fields of psychology and genetics are necessary so that sorting out of the abilities and personalities of children is possible with which the real training or education is possible. He says:

> Thus, the most important thing that a Professor of Educational Foresight could do is to foresee the child's future development --- what he is likely to do well, what place he can take in the social scheme --- to foresee and to plan his training accordingly. It is only on condition of such foresight that our educational system can become efficient. Mr. J.B.S. Haldane is of opinion that 'if psychologists are allowed anything like a free hand and co-operate with geneticists' the sorting out of

children's abilities and potentialities
should become possible 'in the
course of the next century.'
It is certainly not possible now.
(BW: 133)

Huxley says that only a professor should suggest the most efficient system of intellectual and moral training, because there are too many systems in the educational field, but there is no concrete evidence to prove that a particular system is the most effective. So, until a professor suggests, no exemplary system can be formulated. Huxley says that the only way to have such a system is to implement the method of formulating the style of giving training according to the necessity and capacity of every child and keep a record of them on the development of their learning capacities and other related abilities. He says that the intellectual achievements, the propelling discipline, and emotional development of children are to be watched throughout their lives, which is implementable, only with a great passion from the teachers and professors. Huxley says that without such an intelligent system real intelligence cannot be produced and all that any professor of high efficiency and dedication can do is to be fanciful about the talent of children and be optimistic about their bright future like the parents.

Huxley recommends that a professors of foresight must look for any reference from the past prescriptions in the department of social organisation. The general Education Policy must depend on the attitude of the professors towards education and must be clear whether the future society is going to be communistic, is the government going to be decentralized or not and is the family system to be abolished or preserved. Huxley says that answering these questions are very important and that unless there is a plan for men and women, plans and dreams for children are not at all possible. Huxley says:

> Professors of Foresight would be unable to make plans for education without previous reference to the plans of their colleagues in the department of social organization. Is the future society to be communist society or a 'distributive state' of small owners? Is government to be a centralised dictatorship or a federation of small local autonomies? Is the family to be preserved, or is it to be, as far as possible, abolished? Upon the answer to these and similar questions of general policy must depend the attitude of our Professors of Foresight towards education. You cannot make plans for children before you have made plans for men and women. (BW: 133)

Huxley comes to talk of the national and international problems, which are connected to the field of education. He says that professors must foresee the danger of war, and they must think of reforming the teaching of history with an intention of minimizing the dangerous aspects of nationalist propaganda. Professors are asked to predict the dangers of superstition and the unscientific attitude and approach towards the subject of biology at school level, because it is difficult to have a scientific approach to what is so dear. Huxley also talks of the danger of leisure time and says that it must be used for improving the potentialities of children and that the professors of foresight must prepare the children for their significant leisure times also.

Huxley says that the modern man has become more aware of individuals than the ancient man. People have become conscious about the rights of other people with the rampant nature of humanism, which has very profound effect in the realm of family life. So, the modern man has become highly individualistic in thinking and approaches towards things in general and so he cannot embrace the traditional unquestioned beliefs. The divine association with family is no more believable to the modern man. 'Scepticism', the offspring of 'individualism', is further strengthened by 'humanitarianism'. Modern people are not only concerned with their rights but also for their children's. They think of the rights of their children and think that they should not be compelled to do anything, and they should not be tortured in the name of bringing them into a discipline.

The thought that has become evolutionary in the field of education is that the real purpose of education is to offer the guarantee to every child the feasibility of self-expression. Parents, being rational about the children's rights, think of their rights and freedom also and so they do not want to bear the weight of their family responsibilities and want to live life for themselves. Parents, in their attempts to reduce their family responsibilities, reduce the size of their family and handover their children to professional experts to make them very talented professionals in the chosen fields. Huxley says:

> But it is not only the attitude of the parents towards their children that has changed; their attitude towards themselves is no longer the same as in the past. Self-consciously individualistic as well as humanitarianism, parents feel that they too have rights. They want to 'live their own lives', 'to express themselves', to have some other than a merely parental *raison d'etre*. In a word, they resent the weight of family responsibilities. Accordingly, they try to mitigate these responsibilities, first by reducing the size of their families and, secondly, by handling over such children as they do produce to professional educators. (BW: 48)

The pleasure and pride of the past family structure and the number of family members are no more in the present century. In the past, for many generations together, a vast family with many a member, lived under one roof. Huxley expresses his exercised state of mind that family, as a structure has become like a single oak tree from a multi-branched banyan tree, because of the increased concern of the modern parents on their children and on themselves also. There are other causes like economic condition and the aspiration to lead a rich and sophisticated life, which is not possible with many children. He says:

> The family has decreased in size. Increasing individuality and self-conscious rendered intolerable the old, united family with its three or four generations living under the same roof. From being a banyan, the family tree has long since become (at any rate in the West) an oak. Scattered at a distance from the parental stem the acorns grow up into a separate existence. In the past these separate young trees were prolific; but recently the increase of self-conscious individuality has led, for the reasons already given to a reduction in the number of offspring. These psychological causes have been reinforced by economic causes – themselves, very often, of psychological origin. Thus, families cannot be big because we must keep up the standard of living. (BW: 48)

Huxley says that the plan of the elders in reducing the size of the family for various reasons are actually against the wish of their children. No child is happy about being a only child of a family. Children have an inbuilt desire to be surrounded with other children and loving people. A big family has many advantages in child-rearing, and it is the only prescription for the overall healthy psychological development of children. To be a part of a very big family itself gives the psychological impression that you are an inseparable part of the society, learning and mastering the art of being flexible to others. Children brought up in such a family atmosphere need not undergo any training on how to face the world, when they are out of their schools and colleges, since the very family plays the role of the rest of the world, producing confident, understanding, flexible and daring children. Aldous Huxley says that a only child is a highly crippled child in many ways and that even two children are not a better state and having four or five members in a family is a very satisfactory state.

The implied comprehension must be that the majority of the families of the modern world is not satisfactory, which has necessitated the role of a professional educator. The professional educator creates an atmosphere, which is equal to that of the family's that makes the children feel as if they are of one family and ultimately, they experience a psychological satisfaction. It is very shocking when Huxley says that there are people, who call themselves advanced in the modern world, unknowingly advocate the abolition of family system through suggesting that the professional educator shoulders the responsibilities of taking care of the children from their very infancy state. Huxley says that this view is a potential threat to the noble existence of the time-honoured instinct to be gregarious through sentiments and affectionate bonds. A society that is free of any sort of sentimental and affectionate relational bond, is bound to head towards a dangerous and self-devastating selfishness that eventually leads to destruct the rest also. Huxley says:

> Now, from the point of view of the children, small families are not much good. A big family is the world in miniature; to be brought up in a big family is a complete preparation for life. An only child is heavily handicapped. Two children are not very much better off. A family only begins to be really, satisfactory when it can count at least four or five members. From the children's point of view very few modern families are satisfactory. Hence the importance in modern life of the professional educator, who forms an artificial family, within which it is possible for children to find psychological satisfaction. 'Advanced' people propose that the family system should be abolished altogether and that the professional educator, paid by the state, should

take control from earliest infancy. Indeed, this view threatens to become the orthodoxy of the modern democratic State. (BW: 48-49)

Huxley says that the insecurity of a state depends on the number of self-conscious individuals. He says that being humanistic is the only cure for this ailment of not caring for others intimately through the negation of their fundamental duties to the family, which shall protest against all sorts of establishments, including the society, government, country and freedom. Huxley says that human standardization is sure to become a political necessity. Huxley comes out with an optimistic note that family as an institution shall never be perished permanently, since it gives immense psychological contentment, but it is not to be denied that presently there is a potential peril, waiting to wipe off the family system from the society.

Primary Sources

Huxley, Aldous. *Between the Wars*. Chicago, Ivan R. Dee, 1994. Print.

---. *Complete Essay*. 1 Vol. Chicago: Ivan R. Dee, 2000. Print.

---. Collected Essays. London: Chatto and Windus, 1960. Print.

Russell, Bertrand, Fact and Fiction,

---. *Mortals and Others*. 1Vol. London: George Allen & Unwin, London, 1975. Print.

---. *Unpopular Essays*. London: George Allen & Unwin, 1950. Print.

---. *The Basic Writings of Bertrand Russell*. London: George Allen & Unwin, 1961. Print.

---. *Human Society in Ethics and Politics*. London: George Allen & Unwin, 1954. Print.

Secondary Sources

Aiken, L.W. *Bertrand Russell's Philosophy of Morals*. New York: Humanities Press, 1963. Print.

Black, Kenneth and j Harry Ruja. *Bibliography of Bertrand Russell*. Vol. London: Routledge, 1994. Print.

Black well, K. *The Spinojistic Ethics of Bertrand Russell*. London: Allen and Unwin, 1985. Print.

Barker, Chris. *The Sage Dictionary of Cultural Studies*. London: Sage Publications, 2004. Print.

Black, Scot. *Of Essays and Reading in Early Modern Britain.* New York: Palgrave Macmillan, 2006. Print.

Bloom, Herold. *Bloom's Modern Critical Views, Aldous Huxley.* New York: Infobase Publishing, 2010. Print.

Bone, Andrew G. *Détente or Destruction, 1955-57.* Vol. 29. London: Routledge, 2005. Print.

Carr, Brian. *Bertrand Russell, An Introduction.* London: George Allen & Unwin, 1975. Print.

Carrington, Erasmus. *Encyclopedia of Educational Theory and Philosophy.* 1 Vol. 2014. Print.

Charles, Holms M. *Now More Than Ever: Proceedings of the Aldous Huxley Centenary Symposium.* New York: Routledge, 1994. Print.

Chomsky, Noam. *Towards a New Cold War, US foreign policy from Vietnam to Reagan.* New York: The New Press, 2003. Print.

Cooper, David E. *World Philosophies, an Historical Introduction.* Second Edition. New Jersey: Blackwell publishing, 2003. Print.

Davies, Tony. *Humanism.* New York: Routledge, 2008. Print.

Davies, C James. *Human Nature in Politics the dynamics of political behaviour.* New York: John Wiley & sons. 1963. Print.

Deery, June. *Aldous Huxley and the Mysticism of Science.* London: MacMillan, 1996. Print.

Daedalus. *Science and Technology in Contemporary Society.* London: The MIT Press, 1962. Print.

Dyson, A.E. *Aldous Huxley and the Two Nothings*. London: George Allen & Unwin Ltd, 1975. Print.

Egner, Robert E. *Russell's Best*. London: Routledge, 2006. Print.

Eulau, Heinz. Political Behaviour Reader in Theory and Research. New York: Amerind Publishing Co. Pvt. Ltd, 1956. Print.

Firchow, Petre. *Aldous Huxley Satirist and Novelist*. Minneapolils: University of Minnesota Press, 1972. Print.

Fromm, Erich. *Man for Himself*. London: Rouledge, 2003. Print.

Grayling, A C., *Russell. A Very Short Introduction*. Oxford University Press, New York, 2002. Print.

Harris, William. *The New Columbia encyclopaedia*. New York: Columbia University Press, 1995. Print.

Huxley, Julian. *Aldous Huxley, A Momoral Valume*. London: Chatto & Windus, 1965. Print.

Huxley, Aldous. *The Science News-Letter*, Vol. 55, No. 13 (Mar. 26, 1949), pp. 199-202. Society for Science & the Public, 1949. Print.

---. *Brave New World*. London: Cahatto & Windus, 1959. Print.

---. *Improving College and University Teaching*. 6 Vol. Taylor and Francis Ltd., 1958. Print.

---. *An Encylopaedia of Pacifism*. London: Chatto & Windus, 1937. Print.

Honderich, Ted. *The Oxford Companion to Philosophy. Second Edition*. Oxford University Press, 2005. Print.

Jha, Animdha. *Social Philosophy of Bertrand Russell*. Delhi: A Janta Publications, 1978. Print

Jebb, R.C. *The Romanes Lecture, Humanism in Education*. London: Macmillan & Co., Limited, 1899. Print.

Johnson, Samuel. *Dictionary of the English Language*. First Edition. London: Studio Edns, 1994. Print.

Jalalul ha. *Bertrand Russell's Philosophy of Perception*. Delhi: Amar Printing Press, 1984. Print.

Kindersley, Dorling. *Chronicle of the 20ᵗʰ Century*. London: 1988. Print.

Krishnamurti, Jiddu. *To Be Human*. Chennai: Sri Venkareshwara Printing House, 2007. Print.

---. *On relationship*. Chennai: The Indcom Press, 2010. Print.

Marion Young, Iris. *Political Theory: An Overview*. New York: Oxford University Press. 1998. Print.

Mandelbaum, Michael. *The Ideas that Conquered the World, Peace, Democracy, and Free Markets in the Twenty-first Century*. New Delhi: Viva Books Private Limited, 2004. Print.

Mises, Von Ludwig. *Omnipotent Government: The Rise of the Total State and Total War*. New York: Libertarian Press, 1985. Print.

Monk, Ray. Bertrand Russell, The Spirit of Solitude. London: Jonathan Cape, 1996. Print.

Moorehead, Caroline. *Bertrand Russell, A Biography*.
London: Sinclair-Stevenson, 1992. Print.

Murray, Niccolas. *Aldous Huxley, An English Intellectual*,
London: Little Brown & Co, 2009. Print.

Marovitz, Sanford E. *Aldous Huxley and the Nuclear Age:
"Ape and Essence" in Context*. London: Indiana University
Press, 2016. Print.

Nietzsche, Friedzsche. *Thus Spoke Zarathustra*. New York:
Penguin Books, 1995. Print.

Parsons, Talcott. *American Journal of Sociology*. 5 Vol.
Chicago: The Chicago Press, 1938. Print.

Pigden, Charles R. *Russell on Ethics.* London: Routledge,
1999. Print.

Radhakrishnan. *Science, Culture and Man, Impact of scientific
progress on culture and human evolution.* Delhi: Sri Jainendra
Press, 1963. Print.

---. *The Concept of Man, A Study in Comparative Philosophy*.
Delhi: Motilal Banarsodass Publishers Private Limited, 1992.
Print.

Raju, P.T. *The Concept of Man, A Study in Comparative
Philosophy*. Chennai:
Sri Venkareshwara Printing House, 2007. Print.

Rhind Joy, Charles. *Albert Schweitzer: An Anthology*. Boston:
Beacon Press, 1947. Print.

Roberts, W. George. Bertrand Russell Memorial Volume.
George Allen & Unwin, London: 1979. Print.

Russell, Bertrand. *Authority and the Individual*. New York: Routledge, 1985. Print.

---. *Autobiography*. New York: Routledge, 2010. Print.

---. The Ancestry of Fascism. Let the People Think. London: Watts & Co, 1941. Print.

Ryan, Alan. Bertrand Russell: A Political Life. Harmondsworth: Penguin, 1988. Print. Russell, Bertrand. *Power: A New Analysis*. Hyderabad: George Allen & Unwin, 1938. Print.

Sainsbuty, Mark. Bertrand Russell. Philosopher of the Century. London: George Allen & Unwin, 1979.

Santayana, George. *The Birth of Reason and other Essays*. New York: Columbia University Press, 1968. Print.

Satre, Jean Paul. *Existentialism Is a Humanism*. New Haven: Yale University Press, 2007. Print

Schmerl, Rudolf B. *Chicago Review*, 1Vol. Chicago: Chicago Review Press, 1959. Print.

Shashi. *Encyclopaedia of Humanities and Social Sciences*, Volume 49. 1992. Anmol publications, 1992. Print.

Singh, Amita. *The Political Philosophy of Bertrand Russell*. Delhi: Mittal Publications, 1987. Print.

Slater, John G. *Bertrand Russell*. Bristol, England: Thoemmes Press.1994. Print.

Spinks, Lee. *Friedrich Nietzsche*. New York: Routledge Taylor & Francis Group, 2003. Print.

Smith Glenn. *The Phi Delta Kappan*, 9 Vol. Phi Delta Kappa International, 1968. Print.

Swami Vivekananda. *The Complete Works of Swami Vivekananda*. 9 Vols. Kolkata: Advaita Ashrama, 2009. Print.

The Essay Review: A Journal for Literary Criticism of the Nonfiction Essay, Volume I Issue I Spring Action Printing, 2013.

The Quarterly Review of Biology, 4 Vol. The University of Chicago Press, 1946. Print.

Vellacott, Jo. *Bertrand Russell and the Pacifists in the First World War*. New York: St. Martin's Press, 1981.

Watt, Donald. Huxley, Aldous. *The Critical Heritage*. New York: Routledge, 1997. Print.

Watts Estrich, Helen. *The Sewanee Review*. Vol. 47. Johns Hopkins University Press, 1939. Print.

Worley D. Robert. *Bertrand Russell's Power: A New Social Analysis*. New York: Johns Hopkins University, 2021. Print

Journals

Boswell, James. 'The Life of Samuel Johnson' (1791) vol. 2, p. 219 (13 April 1773) 1930, The Conquest of Happiness by Bertrand Russell, Chapter 14: Work, Quote Page 208, George Allen & Unwin, London.

Chmerl, Rudolf B. "Aldous Huxley's Social Criticism." *Chicago Review*, vol. 13, no. 1, 1959, pp. 37–58. *JSTOR*, https://doi.org/10.2307/25293502. Accessed 10 Jan. 2023.

Eagleton, Clyde. "The Demand for World Government." *The American Journal of International Law*, vol. 40, no. 2, 1946,

pp. 390–94. JSTOR. https://doi.org/10.2307/2193199.
Accessed 30 Dec. 2022

Kavka, Gregory S. "Nuclear Weapons and World
Government." *The Monist*, vol. 70, no.   3, 1987, pp. 298–
315. JSTOR, http://www.jstor.org/stable/27903036. Accessed
30 Dec. 2022.

Meclier, Jerome. "Aldous Huxley: Dystopian Essayist of the
1930s." *Utopian Studies*, vol. 7, no. 2, 1996, pp. 196–212.
JSTOR, http://www.jstor.org/stable/20719517. Accessed 19
Jan. 2023.

 Meckier, Jerome. "Prepping for Brave New World: Aldous
Huxley's Essays of the   1920s." *Utopian Studies*, vol. 12,
no. 2, 2001, pp. 234–45. *JSTOR*,
http://www.jstor.org/stable/20718327. Accessed 19 Jan. 2023.

Remphel, Richard. *Pacifism and Revolution* (1916-18),
Collected Papers, Vol. 14, Routledge, London and New York:
1995.

Roosevelt, Franklin D. (1950). "Public Papers of the
Presidents of the United States: F.D. Roosevelt, 1944-1945,
Volume 13", p.615, Best Books on.

Smith, Glenn. "Aldous Huxley: Analyst and Prophet for
Twentieth Century Man." *The   Phi Delta Kappan*, vol.
49, no. 9, 1968, pp. 507–10. *JSTOR*,
http://www.jstor.org/stable/20372148. Accessed 19 Jan. 2023.

Yunker, James A. "Evolutionary World Government." *Peace
Research*, vol. 44, no. 1,   2012, pp. 95–96. JSTOR,
http://www.jstor.org/stable/23607919. Accessed 30   Dec.
2022.

Electronic Resources

So You Want to Read Bertrand Russell.pdf

ON SUFFERING AND COMPASSION.pdf

file:///F:/MY%20goal/article%20pacifism_brief.pdf

http://theessayreview.org/

file:///F:/MY%20goal/TheEssayReviewVolume1Issue1.pdf

https://www.spokesmanbooks.com/Spokesman/PDF/140Russe
ll.pdf

https://humanists.uk/wp-
content/uploads/ExploringHumanism-Course.pdf

https://americanhumanist.org/

file:///C:/Users/HAPPY1/Downloads/1277-Article%20Text-
4247-1-10-20201125.pdf